OECD/G20 Base Erosion and Profit Shifting Project

Limiting Base Erosion Involving Interest Deductions and Other Financial Payments, Action 4 - 2015 Final Report

OECD

BETTER POLICIES FOR BETTER LIVES

This document and any map included herein are without prejudice to the status of or sovereignty over any territory, to the delimitation of international frontiers and boundaries and to the name of any territory, city or area.

Please cite this publication as:
OECD (2015), *Limiting Base Erosion Involving Interest Deductions and Other Financial Payments, Action 4 - 2015 Final Report*, OECD/G20 Base Erosion and Profit Shifting Project, OECD Publishing, Paris.
http://dx.doi.org/10.1787/9789264241176-en

ISBN 978-92-64-24116-9 (print)
ISBN 978-92-64-24117-6 (PDF)

Series: OECD/G20 Base Erosion and Profit Shifting Project
ISSN 2313-2604 (print)
ISSN 2313-2612 (online)

Photo credits: Cover © ninog – Fotolia.com

Corrigenda to OECD publications may be found on line at: *www.oecd.org/about/publishing/corrigenda.htm*.

Foreword

International tax issues have never been as high on the political agenda as they are today. The integration of national economies and markets has increased substantially in recent years, putting a strain on the international tax rules, which were designed more than a century ago. Weaknesses in the current rules create opportunities for base erosion and profit shifting (BEPS), requiring bold moves by policy makers to restore confidence in the system and ensure that profits are taxed where economic activities take place and value is created.

Following the release of the report *Addressing Base Erosion and Profit Shifting* in February 2013, OECD and G20 countries adopted a 15-point Action Plan to address BEPS in September 2013. The Action Plan identified 15 actions along three key pillars: introducing coherence in the domestic rules that affect cross-border activities, reinforcing substance requirements in the existing international standards, and improving transparency as well as certainty.

Since then, all G20 and OECD countries have worked on an equal footing and the European Commission also provided its views throughout the BEPS project. Developing countries have been engaged extensively via a number of different mechanisms, including direct participation in the Committee on Fiscal Affairs. In addition, regional tax organisations such as the African Tax Administration Forum, the *Centre de rencontre des administrations fiscales* and the *Centro Interamericano de Administraciones Tributarias*, joined international organisations such as the International Monetary Fund, the World Bank and the United Nations, in contributing to the work. Stakeholders have been consulted at length: in total, the BEPS project received more than 1 400 submissions from industry, advisers, NGOs and academics. Fourteen public consultations were held, streamed live on line, as were webcasts where the OECD Secretariat periodically updated the public and answered questions.

After two years of work, the 15 actions have now been completed. All the different outputs, including those delivered in an interim form in 2014, have been consolidated into a comprehensive package. The BEPS package of measures represents the first substantial renovation of the international tax rules in almost a century. Once the new measures become applicable, it is expected that profits will be reported where the economic activities that generate them are carried out and where value is created. BEPS planning strategies that rely on outdated rules or on poorly co-ordinated domestic measures will be rendered ineffective.

Implementation therefore becomes key at this stage. The BEPS package is designed to be implemented via changes in domestic law and practices, and via treaty provisions, with negotiations for a multilateral instrument under way and expected to be finalised in 2016. OECD and G20 countries have also agreed to continue to work together to ensure a consistent and co-ordinated implementation of the BEPS recommendations. Globalisation requires that global solutions and a global dialogue be established which go beyond OECD and G20 countries. To further this objective, in 2016 OECD and G20 countries will conceive an inclusive framework for monitoring, with all interested countries participating on an equal footing.

A better understanding of how the BEPS recommendations are implemented in practice could reduce misunderstandings and disputes between governments. Greater focus on implementation and tax administration should therefore be mutually beneficial to governments and business. Proposed improvements to data and analysis will help support ongoing evaluation of the quantitative impact of BEPS, as well as evaluating the impact of the countermeasures developed under the BEPS Project.

Table of contents

Boxes

Figures

Tables

Abbreviations and acronyms

BEPS	Base Erosion and Profit Shifting
BIAC	Business and Industry Advisory Committee
CFC	Controlled Foreign Company
CIV	Collective Investment Vehicle
EBIT	Earnings before interest and taxes
EBITDA	Earnings before interest, taxes, depreciation and amortisation
EU	European Union
GAAP	Generally Accepted Accounting Principles
IFRS	International Financial Reporting Standards
JV	Joint Venture
OECD	Organisation for Economic Co-operation and Development
PwC	PricewaterhouseCoopers
TFEU	Treaty on the Functioning of the European Union
USD	United States Dollar

Executive summary

It is an empirical matter of fact that money is mobile and fungible. Thus, multinational groups may achieve favourable tax results by adjusting the amount of debt in a group entity. The influence of tax rules on the location of debt within multinational groups has been established in a number of academic studies and it is well known that groups can easily multiply the level of debt at the level of individual group entities via intra-group financing. Financial instruments can also be used to make payments which are economically equivalent to interest but have a different legal form, therefore escaping restrictions on the deductibility of interest. Base Erosion and Profit Shifting (BEPS) risks in this area may arise in three basic scenarios:

- Groups placing higher levels of third party debt in high tax countries.
- Groups using intragroup loans to generate interest deductions in excess of the group's actual third party interest expense.
- Groups using third party or intragroup financing to fund the generation of tax exempt income.

To address these risks, Action 4 of the *Action Plan on Base Erosion and Profit Shifting* (BEPS Action Plan, OECD, 2013) called for recommendations regarding best practices in the design of rules to prevent base erosion through the use of interest expense. This report analyses several best practices and recommends an approach which directly addresses the risks outlined above. The recommended approach is based on a fixed ratio rule which limits an entity's net deductions for interest and payments economically equivalent to interest to a percentage of its earnings before interest, taxes, depreciation and amortisation (EBITDA). As a minimum this should apply to entities in multinational groups. To ensure that countries apply a fixed ratio that is low enough to tackle BEPS, while recognising that not all countries are in the same position, the recommended approach includes a corridor of possible ratios of between 10% and 30%. The report also includes factors which countries should take into account in setting their fixed ratio within this corridor. The approach can be supplemented by a worldwide group ratio rule which allows an entity to exceed this limit in certain circumstances.

Recognising that some groups are highly leveraged with third party debt for non-tax reasons, the recommended approach proposes a group ratio rule alongside the fixed ratio rule. This would allow an entity with net interest expense above a country's fixed ratio to deduct interest up to the level of the net interest/EBITDA ratio of its worldwide group. Countries may also apply an uplift of up to 10% to the group's net third party interest expense to prevent double taxation. The earnings-based worldwide group ratio rule can also be replaced by different group ratio rules, such as the "equity escape" rule (which compares an entity's level of equity and assets to those held by its group) currently in place in some countries. A country may also choose not to introduce any group ratio rule. If a country does not introduce a group ratio rule, it should apply the fixed ratio rule to entities in multinational and domestic groups without improper discrimination.

The recommended approach will mainly impact entities with both a high level of net interest expense and a high net interest/EBITDA ratio, in particular where the entity's ratio is higher than that of its worldwide group. This is a straightforward approach and ensures that an entity's net interest deductions are directly linked to the taxable income generated by its economic activities. An important feature of the fixed ratio rule is that it only limits an entity's net interest deductions (i.e. interest expense in excess of interest income). The rule does not restrict the ability of multinational groups to raise third party debt centrally in the country and entity which is most efficient taking into account non-tax factors such as credit rating, currency and access to capital markets, and then on-lend the borrowed funds within the group to where it is used to fund the group's economic activities.

The recommended approach also allows countries to supplement the fixed ratio rule and group ratio rule with other provisions that reduce the impact of the rules on entities or situations which pose less BEPS risk, such as:

- A *de minimis* threshold which carves-out entities which have a low level of net interest expense. Where a group has more than one entity in a country, it is recommended that the threshold be applied to the total net interest expense of the local group.
- An exclusion for interest paid to third party lenders on loans used to fund public-benefit projects, subject to conditions. In these circumstances, an entity may be highly leveraged but, due to the nature of the projects and the close link to the public sector, the BEPS risk is reduced.
- The carry forward of disallowed interest expense and/or unused interest capacity (where an entity's actual net interest deductions are below the maximum permitted) for use in future years. This will reduce the impact of earnings volatility on the ability of an entity to deduct interest expense. The carry forward of disallowed interest expense will also help entities which incur interest expenses on long-term investments that are expected to generate taxable income only in later years, and will allow entities with losses to claim interest deductions when they return to profit.

The report also recommends that the approach be supported by targeted rules to prevent its circumvention, for example by artificially reducing the level of net interest expense. It also recommends that countries consider introducing rules to tackle specific BEPS risks not addressed by the recommended approach, such as where an entity without net interest expense shelters interest income.

Finally, the report recognises that the banking and insurance sectors have specific features which must be taken into account and therefore there is a need to develop suitable and specific rules that address BEPS risks in these sectors.

Further technical work will be conducted on specific areas of the recommended approach, including the detailed operation of the worldwide group ratio rule and the specific rules to address risks posed by banking and insurance groups. This work is expected to be completed in 2016.

The amount of intragroup interest and payments economically equivalent to interest is also affected by transfer pricing rules. Revisions to Chapter I of the Transfer Pricing Guidelines for Multinational Enterprises and Tax Administrations under Actions 8-10 of the BEPS Action Plan (OECD, 2013), contained in the OECD Report *Aligning Transfer*

Pricing Outcomes with Value Creation (OECD, 2015), limit the amount of interest payable to group companies lacking appropriate substance to no more than a risk-free return on the funding provided and require group synergies to be taken into account when evaluating intragroup financial payments. Further work on the transfer pricing aspects of financial transactions will be undertaken during 2016 and 2017.

A co-ordinated implementation of the recommended approach will successfully impact on the ability of multinational groups to use debt to achieve BEPS outcomes. To ensure the recommended approach remains effective in tackling BEPS involving interest, the implementation, operation and impact of the approach will be monitored over time, to allow for a comprehensive and informed review as necessary.

Introduction

Use of interest and payments economically equivalent to interest for base erosion and profit shifting

1. The use of third party and related party interest is perhaps one of the most simple of the profit-shifting techniques available in international tax planning. The fluidity and fungibility of money makes it a relatively simple exercise to adjust the mix of debt and equity in a controlled entity. Against this background, Action 4 of the *Action Plan on Base Erosion and Profit Shifting* (BEPS Action Plan, OECD, 2013) calls for the:

> *[development of] recommendations regarding best practices in the design of rules to prevent base erosion through the use of interest expense, for example through the use of related-party and third-party debt to achieve excessive interest deductions or to finance the production of exempt or deferred income, and other financial payments that are economically equivalent to interest payments. The work will evaluate the effectiveness of different types of limitations. In connection with and in support of the foregoing work, transfer pricing guidance will also be developed regarding the pricing of related party financial transactions, including financial and performance guarantees, derivatives (including internal derivatives used in intra-bank dealings), and captive and other insurance arrangements. The work will be co-ordinated with the work on hybrids and CFC rules.*

2. Most countries tax debt and equity differently for the purposes of their domestic law. Interest on debt is generally a deductible expense of the payer and taxed at ordinary rates in the hands of the payee. Dividends, or other equity returns, on the other hand, are generally not deductible and are typically subject to some form of tax relief (an exemption, exclusion, credit, etc.) in the hands of the payee. While, in a purely domestic context, these differences in treatment may result in debt and equity being subject to a similar overall tax burden, the difference in the treatment of the payer creates a tax-induced bias, in the cross-border context, towards debt financing. The distortion is compounded by tax planning techniques that may be employed to reduce or eliminate tax on interest income in the jurisdiction of the payee.

3. In the cross-border context, the main tax policy concerns surrounding interest deductions relate to the debt funding of outbound and inbound investment by groups. Parent companies are typically able to claim relief for their interest expense while the return on equity holdings is taxed on a preferential basis, benefiting from a participation exemption, preferential tax rate or taxation only on distribution. On the other hand, subsidiary entities may be heavily debt financed, using excessive deductions on intragroup loans to shelter local profits from tax. Taken together, these opportunities surrounding inbound and outbound investment potentially create competitive distortions between groups operating internationally and those operating in the domestic market. This has a negative impact on capital ownership neutrality, creating a tax preference for assets to be held by multinational groups rather than domestic groups.[1] In addition, as identified in the BEPS Action Plan (OECD, 2013), when groups exploit these opportunities, it reduces the revenues available to

governments and affects the integrity of the tax system. The use of interest deductions to fund income which is exempt or deferred for tax purposes, and obtaining relief for interest deductions greater than the actual net interest expense of the group, can also contribute to other forms of base erosion and profit shifting. These include the use of intragroup loans to generate deductible interest expense in high tax jurisdictions and interest income in low or no tax jurisdictions; the development of hybrid instruments which give rise to deductible interest expense but no corresponding taxable income; and the use of loans to invest in assets which give rise to a return that is not taxed or is taxed at a reduced rate. Box 1 below contains simple examples of how a multinational group can generate a benefit based on the location of its debt, in both outbound and inbound investment scenarios.

Box 1. Example of the impact of tax on the location of interest expense[2]

These examples assume no restriction on the ability of a group to obtain deductions for its interest expense, for example under transfer pricing or thin capitalisation rules.

Outbound investment

Consider a simple group structure, including two companies (A Co and B Co). A Co is resident in a country with a 35% rate of corporate income tax, which exempts foreign source dividends from tax. B Co is resident in a country with a 15% corporate tax rate.

B Co borrows USD 100 from a third party bank at an interest rate of 10%.[3] B Co uses these funds in its business and generates additional operating profit of USD 15. After deducting the USD 10 interest cost, B Co has a pre-tax profit of USD 5 and a post-tax profit of USD 4.25.

Alternatively, A Co could borrow the USD 100 from the bank and contribute the same amount to B Co as equity. In this case, B Co has no interest expense and its full operating profit of USD 15 is subject to tax. B Co now has a pre-tax profit of USD 15 and a post-tax profit of USD 12.75. Assuming A Co can set its interest expense against other income, A Co has a pre-tax cost of USD 10 and a post-tax cost of USD 6.50. Taken together, A Co and B Co have a total pre-tax profit from the transaction of USD 5 and a total post-tax profit of USD 6.25.

As a result of transferring the interest expense from B Co to A Co, the group is now subject to a negative effective rate of taxation (i.e. the group's post-tax profit exceeds its pre-tax profit).

Inbound investment

A similar result can also be achieved in an inbound investment context.

In this case, A Co is resident in a country with a 15% rate of corporate income tax and B Co is resident in a country with a 35% corporate tax rate.

B Co borrows USD 100 from a third party bank at an interest rate of 10%. B Co uses these funds in its business and generates additional operating profit of USD 15. After deducting the USD 10 interest cost, B Co has a pre-tax profit of USD 5 and a post-tax profit of USD 3.25.

A Co could also replace USD 50 of existing equity in B Co with a loan of the same amount, at an interest rate of 10% (the same rate as on the loan from the third party bank). In this case, B Co has a pre-tax and post-tax profit of nil. A Co has interest income on its loan to B Co, and has a pre-tax profit of USD 5 and a post-tax profit of USD 4.25. The group has reduced its effective tax rate from 35% to 15% by shifting profit from B Co to A Co.

Taking this one step further, A Co could replace USD 100 of existing equity in B Co with a loan of the same amount. Assuming B Co can set its interest expense against other income, as a result of this transaction B Co now has a pre-tax loss of USD 5 and a post-tax loss of USD 3.25. A Co receives interest income from B Co, and has a pre-tax profit of USD 10 and a post-tax profit of USD 8.50. Taken together, A Co and B Co have a pre-tax profit of USD 5 and a post-tax profit of USD 5.25. As a result of thinly capitalising B Co and shifting profit to A Co, the group is now subject to a negative effective rate of taxation.

4. The ongoing existence of international debt shifting has been established in a number of academic studies which show that groups leverage more debt in subsidiaries located in high tax countries (Møen et al., 2011; Huizinga, Laeven and Nicodeme, 2008; Mintz and Weichenrieder, 2005; Desai, Foley and Hines, 2004). Debt shifting does not only impact developed countries, but is also an issue for developing countries which, according to academic research, are even more prone to these risks (Fuest, Hebous and Riedel, 2011). Academics have shown that thin capitalisation is strongly associated with multinational groups (Taylor and Richardson, 2013), and that foreign-owned businesses use more debt than comparable domestically-owned businesses (Egger et al., 2010). Additional debt is provided through both intragroup and third party debt (Møen et al., 2011), with intragroup loans typically used in cases where the borrowing costs on third party debt are high (Buettner et al., 2012). Academics have also looked at the effectiveness of thin capitalisation rules and illustrated that such rules have the effect of reducing the total debt of subsidiaries (Blouin et al., 2014; Buettner et al., 2012). Where thin capitalisation rules apply solely to interest deductions on intragroup debt, these rules are effective in reducing intragroup debt but then lead to an increase in third party debt, although this may not be to the same extent (Buettner et al., 2012).

5. The impact of interest limitation rules on investment has also been the subject of academic studies and the topic has been approached using both theoretical models and empirical analysis. Analysing the impact of interest limitation rules on investment from a theoretical standpoint, academics suggest that such rules would increase effective capital costs thus reducing real investment (Ruf and Schindler, 2012) The theoretical approach is supported by studies which suggest that certain countries set lenient thin capitalisation rules in order to protect foreign direct investment (Haufer and Runkel, 2012). The limited empirical analysis that has been done does not, however, support this theory. Two studies, both analysing the effect of German interest limitation rules on investment, find no significant evidence of a reduction of investment in relation to either thin capitalisation rules (Weichenrieder and Windischbauer, 2008) or interest barrier rules based on a ratio of interest expense to income (Buslei and Simmler, 2012).[4] This lack of empirical support may be due to a number of factors including the fact that multinational groups may avoid the application of the interest limitation rule by using loopholes in the legislation or by adjusting their capital structure (Ruf and Schindler, 2012). Therefore, there does not seem to be enough empirical evidence to reach conclusions on the actual impact of interest limitation rules on foreign investment.

6. Countries have introduced a wide range of rules to address issues of base erosion and profit shifting involving third party and intragroup interest. These include general interest limitation rules which put an overall limit on the level of interest deductions that an entity can claim, as well as targeted rules which address specific planning risks. Where general interest limitation rules have been used, in some countries they have focused on inbound investment situations only, while in others rules have attempted to address both inbound and outbound situations. The main types of rules applied by countries are considered later in this introduction. These approaches have been successful to varying degrees, but there is a sense that unilateral action by countries is failing to tackle some of the issues at the heart of this problem. Partly, this is because the fungibility of money and the flexibility of financial instruments have made it possible for groups to bypass the effect of rules and replicate similar benefits using different tools. This has led to countries repeatedly introducing new rules, or amending existing ones, creating layers of complexity without addressing the key underlying issues. There is also a concern that a robust approach to restrict interest deductions by a single country could adversely impact

the attractiveness of the country to international business and the ability of domestic groups to compete globally.

7. It has therefore become increasingly apparent that a consistent approach utilising international best practices would be a more effective and efficient way of addressing concerns surrounding the use of interest in base erosion and profit shifting. This approach should encourage groups to adopt funding structures whereby: (i) the net interest expense of an entity is linked to the overall net interest expense of the group; and (ii) the distribution of a group's net interest expense should be linked to income-producing activities. Groups should also benefit from a consistent approach between countries. Similar rules based on the same principles should make the operation of rules more predictable, enabling groups to plan their capital structures with greater confidence. It could also make it possible to introduce group-wide systems and processes to produce required information, making compliance with rules in multiple countries simpler and cheaper. A consistent approach should remove distortions, reduce the risk of unintended double taxation and, by removing opportunities for base erosion and profit shifting, improve fairness and equality between groups.

BEPS Action Plan and interest expense

8. In 2012, the G20 called on the Organisation for Economic Co-operation and Development (OECD) to analyse the issue of base erosion and profit shifting and develop an action plan to address these issues in a co-ordinated and comprehensive manner. The BEPS Action Plan (OECD, 2013) was delivered by the OECD in July 2013 and contains 15 actions. Several of these address different aspects of base erosion and profit shifting using interest. Arrangements using hybrid financial instruments or hybrid entities to generate two tax deductions for the same payment, or payments which are deductible in the payer but are not taxed as ordinary income in the recipient, are addressed through model rules developed under Action 2 (Neutralise the effects of hybrid mismatch arrangements). Work under Action 3 (Strengthen CFC rules) has developed recommendations regarding the design of controlled foreign company (CFC) rules, which among other things should help to address the issue of interest income in controlled companies in low tax jurisdictions. Action 4 (Limit base erosion via interest deductions and other financial payments), which is the focus of this report, makes recommendations for best practices in the design of rules to address base erosion and profit shifting using interest and payments economically equivalent to interest, by aligning interest deductions with taxable economic activity. Action 4 also refers to the development of transfer pricing guidance for related party financial transactions, which will be carried out as a separate project to be completed by 2017. This work should in no way impede countries from implementing the best practice approach contained in this report. Revisions to Chapter I of the Transfer Pricing Guidelines for Multinational Enterprises and Tax Administrations under Actions 8-10 (Intangibles; Risks and capital; and Other high risk transactions) limit the amount of interest payable to group companies lacking appropriate substance to no more than a risk-free return on the funding provided and require group synergies to be taken into account when evaluating intragroup financial payments.

9. Action 4 is focused on the use of third party, related party and intragroup debt to achieve excessive interest deductions or to finance the production of exempt or deferred income. A best practice approach to tackling these issues should apply to all forms of interest and payments equivalent to interest, to ensure that groups in an equivalent position are treated consistently and to reduce the risk of a rule being avoided by a group

structuring its borrowings into a different legal form. Base erosion and profit shifting can arise from arrangements using third party debt (e.g. where one entity or country bears an excessive proportion of the group's total net third party interest expense) and intragroup debt (e.g. where a group uses intragroup interest expense to shift taxable income from high tax to low tax countries). It can also occur where payments are made to a lender outside a country or within the same country. For example, within a country base erosion and profit shifting may arise as a result of interest paid to a third party under a structured arrangement, or where interest is paid to a group entity in the same country which makes a corresponding payment to a foreign lender. In order to be effective in tackling base erosion and profit shifting, a best practice approach should therefore apply to all of these situations.

Existing approaches to tackle base erosion and profit shifting involving interest

10. The recommendations in this report are the result of significant work which explored the advantages and disadvantages of different types of rules. This included a review of countries' experiences as to how rules operate in practice and impacts on taxpayer behaviour. It also included an analysis of empirical data on the leverage of groups and entities in countries which do and do not currently apply rules to limit interest deductions, and the results of academic studies.

11. Rules currently applied by countries fall into six broad groups, with some countries using a combined approach that includes more than one type of rule:

1. Arm's length tests, which compare the level of interest or debt in an entity with the position that would have existed had the entity been dealing entirely with third parties.
2. Withholding tax on interest payments, which are used to allocate taxing rights to a source jurisdiction.
3. Rules which disallow a specified percentage of the interest expense of an entity, irrespective of the nature of the payment or to whom it is made.
4. Rules which limit the level of interest expense or debt in an entity with reference to a fixed ratio, such as debt/equity, interest/earnings or interest/total assets.
5. Rules which limit the level of interest expense or debt in an entity with reference to the group's overall position.
6. Targeted anti-avoidance rules which disallow interest expense on specific transactions.

12. An arm's length test requires consideration of an individual entity's circumstances, the amount of debt that the entity would be able to raise from third party lenders and the terms under which that debt could be borrowed. It allows a tax administration to focus on the particular commercial circumstances of an entity or a group but it can be resource intensive and time consuming for both taxpayers and tax administrations to apply. Also, because each entity is considered separately after arrangements are entered into, the outcomes of applying a rule can be uncertain, although this may be reduced through advance agreements with the tax administration. An advantage of an arm's length test is that it recognises that entities may have different levels of interest expense depending on their circumstances. However, some countries with experience of applying such an approach in practice expressed concerns over how

effective it is in preventing base erosion and profit shifting, although it could be a useful complement to other rules (e.g. in pricing the interest income and expense of an entity, before applying interest limitation rules). In particular, countries have experience of groups structuring intragroup debt with equity-like features to justify interest payments significantly in excess of those the group actually incurs on its third party debt. Additionally, an arm's length test does not prevent an entity from claiming a deduction for interest expense which is used to fund investments in non-taxable assets or income streams, which is a base erosion risk specifically mentioned as a concern in the BEPS Action Plan (OECD, 2013).

13. Withholding taxes are primarily used to allocate taxing rights to a source country, but by imposing tax on cross-border payments they may also reduce the benefit to groups from base erosion and profit shifting transactions. Withholding tax has the advantage of being a relatively mechanical tool which is easy to apply and administer. However, unless withholding tax is applied at the same rate as corporate tax, opportunities for base erosion and profit shifting would remain. In fact, in some cases withholding taxes can drive base erosion and profit shifting behaviour, where groups enter into structured arrangements to avoid imposition of a tax or generate additional tax benefits (such as multiple entities claiming credit with respect to tax withheld). Where withholding tax is applied, double taxation can be addressed by giving credit in the country where the payment is received, although the effectiveness of this is reduced if credit is only given up to the amount of tax on net income. This can impose a significant cost on groups not engaged in base erosion and profit shifting, if an entity suffers withholding tax on its gross interest receipts, but is unable to claim a credit for this because its taxable income is reduced by interest expense. In practice, where withholding tax is applied the rate is often reduced (sometimes to zero) under bilateral tax treaties. It would also be extremely difficult for European Union (EU) Member States to apply withholding taxes on interest payments made within the European Union due to the Interest and Royalty Directive.[5] In addition, there are broader policy reasons why some countries do not currently apply withholding tax to interest payments, which could make the introduction of new taxes difficult. Taken together, these factors mean that in many situations withholding taxes would not be a suitable tool for completely tackling the base erosion and profit shifting risks which are the subject of this report. However, countries may still continue to apply withholding tax alongside the best practice.

14. Rules which disallow a percentage of all interest paid by an entity in effect increase the cost of all debt finance above any *de minimis* threshold. Therefore, entities with a relatively low leverage will be subject to the same proportionate disallowance as similar entities with very high levels of debt. This approach is likely to be more effective in reducing the general tax preference for debt over equity, than in targeting base erosion and profit shifting involving interest.

15. For the reasons set out above, the rules in groups 1 to 3, on their own, do not address all of the aims of Action 4 set out in the BEPS Action Plan (OECD, 2013). As such, they are not considered to be best practices in tackling base erosion and profit shifting involving interest and payments economically equivalent to interest if they are not strengthened with other interest limitation rules. However, these rules may still have a role to play within a country's tax system alongside a best practice approach, either in supporting those rules or in meeting other tax policy goals. Therefore, after introducing the best practice approach, a country may also continue to apply an arm's length test, withholding tax on interest, or rules to disallow a percentage of an entity's total interest

expense, so long as these do not reduce the effectiveness of the best practice in tackling base erosion and profit shifting.

16. The best practice approach set out in this report is based on a combination of some or all of the rules in groups 4 to 6 above. A general limit on interest deductions would restrict the ability of an entity to deduct net interest expense based on a fixed financial ratio. This could be combined with a rule to allow the entity to deduct more interest up to the group's equivalent financial ratio where this is higher. If a country does not introduce a group ratio rule, it should apply the fixed ratio rule to entities in multinational and domestic groups without improper discrimination. These general rules should be complemented by targeted rules to address planning to reduce or avoid the effect of the general rules, and targeted rules can also be used to tackle specific risks not covered by the general rules. This approach should provide effective protection for countries against base erosion and profit shifting involving interest, but should not prevent businesses from raising the debt finance necessary for their business and commercial investments.

17. Rules which limit interest expense by reference to a fixed ratio are relatively easy to apply and link the level of interest expense to a measure of an entity's economic activity. These rules are currently applied by a number of countries. However, the way in which existing rules are designed is not always the most effective way to tackle base erosion and profit shifting. The majority of countries applying fixed ratio rules link interest deductibility to the level of equity in an entity, typically through thin capitalisation rules based on a debt/equity test. The main advantage of such a test is that it is relatively easy for tax administrations to obtain relevant information on the level of debt and equity in an entity and it also provides a reasonable level of certainty to groups in planning their financing. However, set against these advantages are a number of important disadvantages. A rule which limits the amount of debt in an entity still allows significant flexibility in terms of the rate of interest that an entity may pay on that debt. Also, an equity test allows entities with higher levels of equity capital to deduct more interest expense, which makes it relatively easy for a group to manipulate the outcome of a test by increasing the level of equity in a particular entity. An illustration of this is included as Example 1 in Annex D. It was therefore agreed by countries involved in this work that fixed ratio debt/equity tests should not be included as a general interest limitation rule within a best practice approach to tackle base erosion and profit shifting, although again this is not intended to suggest that these tests cannot play a role within an overall tax policy to limit interest deductions.

18. In recent years, countries have increasingly introduced fixed ratio tests based on an entity's interest/earnings ratio, which is a better tool to combat base erosion and profit shifting. In these tests, the measure of earnings used is typically earnings before interest, taxes, depreciation and amortisation (EBITDA). Most countries presently use a tax measure of EBITDA. However, there remains a general view that in many cases multinational groups are still able to claim total interest deductions significantly in excess of the group's actual third party interest expense. Available data, discussed in Chapter 6, shows that the majority of publicly traded multinational groups with positive EBITDA have a net third party interest/EBITDA ratio below 10%, based on consolidated financial reporting information.

19. Rules which directly compare the level of interest expense or debt of an entity to that of its group are less common, but are applied by a small number of countries. These group ratio tests currently typically operate by reference to debt/equity ratios. However,

in many cases the amount of equity in an entity may at best only be an indirect measure of its level of activity and as already mentioned can be subject to manipulation.

20. Targeted rules can complement a general interest limitation rule and are therefore a component of the best practice approach. Many countries have targeted anti-avoidance rules and these can be an effective response to specific base erosion and profit shifting risks. However, as new base erosion and profit shifting opportunities are exploited, further targeted rules may be required and so there is a tendency over time for more rules to be introduced, resulting in a complex system and increased administration and compliance costs. An approach which includes an effective general interest limitation rule should reduce the need for additional targeted rules, although some will be required to address specific risks. However, these targeted rules should operate consistently with the general interest limitation rules recommended in this report.

European Union law issues

21. Throughout this work, EU law requirements imposed on Member States of the European Union have been considered, and in particular the need for recommended approaches to be in accordance with EU treaty freedoms, directives and State aid regulations. Although countries outside the European Union are not required to comply with these obligations, the need for a consistent international approach outlined above means that any approach which cannot be fully implemented by the 28 EU Member States is unlikely to be effective in tackling the global issue of base erosion and profit shifting. Specific issues related to EU treaty freedoms, directives and State aid rules and possible approaches to deal with them are set out in Annex A of this report.

Notes

1. A domestic group is a group which operates wholly within a single country.

2. The first part of this example is adapted from Graetz (2008).

3. All monetary amounts in this example are denominated in United States dollars (USD). This is an illustrative example only, and is not intended to reflect a real case or the position in a particular country.

4. Weichenrieder and Windischbauer (2008) analysed the effect of the 1994 introduction and the 2001 tightening of Germany's former thin capitalisation rule. Buslei and Simmler (2012) analysed the effect of the introduction of Germany's current interest limitation rule in 2008.

5. Council Directive 2003/49/EC of 3 June 2003 on a common system of taxation applicable to interest and royalty payments made between associated companies of different Member States [2003] OJ L157/49.

Bibliography

Blouin, J. et al. (2014), "Thin Capitalization Rules and Multinational Firm Capital Structure", *IMF Working Paper*, No. 14/12, International Monetary Fund, Washington, DC.

Buettner, T. et al. (2012), "The impact of thin-capitalization rules on the capital structure of multinational firms", *Journal of Public Economics*, Vol. 96, Elsevier, Amsterdam, pp. 930-938.

Buslei, H. and M. Simmler (2012), "The impact of introducing an interest barrier - Evidence from the German corporation tax reform 2008", *DIW Discussion Papers*, No. 1215, DIW Berlin.

Desai, M.A., C.F. Foley and J.R. Hines (2004), "A Multinational Perspective on Capital Structure Choice and Internal Capital Markets", *The Journal of Finance*, Vol. 59, American Finance Association, pp. 2451-2487.

Egger. P. et al. (2010), "Corporate taxation, debt financing and foreign-plant ownership", *European Economic Review*, Vol. 54, Elsevier, Amsterdam, pp. 96-107.

Fuest, C., S. Hebous and N. Riedel (2011), "International debt shifting and multinational firms in developing economies", *Economic Letters*, Vol. 113, Elsevier, Amsterdam, pp. 135-138.

Graetz, M.J. (2008), "A Multilateral Solution for the Income Tax Treatment of Interest Expenses", *Bulletin for International Taxation*, Vol. 62, IBFD, pp. 486-493.

Haufler, A. and M. Runkel (2012), "Firms' financial choices and thin capitalization rules under corporate tax competition", *European Economic Review*, Vol. 56, Elsevier, Amsterdam, pp. 1087-1103.

Huizinga, H., L. Laeven and G. Nicodeme (2008), "Capital structure and international debt shifting", *Journal of Financial Economics*, Vol. 88, Elsevier, Amsterdam, pp. 80-118.

Mintz, J. and A.J. Weichenrieder (2005), "Taxation and the Financial Structure or German Outbound FDI", *CESifo Working Paper*, No. 1612.

Møen, J. et al. (2011), "International Debt Shifting: Do Multinationals Shift Internal or External Debt?", *University of Konstanz, Department of Economics Working Paper Series*, No. 2011-40.

OECD (2013), *Action Plan on Base Erosion and Profit Shifting*, OECD Publishing, Paris, http://dx.doi.org/10.1787/9789264202719-en.

Ruf, M. and D. Schindler (2012), "Debt Shifting and Thin Capitalization Rules - German Experience and Alternative Approaches", *Norwegian School of Economics, Bergen, NHH Discussion Paper RRR*, No. 06-2012.

Taylor, G. and G. Richardson (2013), "The determinants of thinly capitalized tax avoidance structures: Evidence from Australian firms", *Journal of International Accounting, Auditing and Taxation*, Vol. 22, Elsevier, Amsterdam, pp. 12-25.

Weichenrieder, A.J. and H. Windischbauer (2008), "Thin-capitalization rules and company responses - Experience from German legislation", *CESifo Working Paper*, No. 2456.

Chapter 1

Recommendations for a best practice approach

22. The critical objective of the work on Action 4 is to identify coherent and consistent solutions to address base erosion and profit shifting using interest and payments economically equivalent to interest. In constructing the best practice approach described in this report, a focus has been placed on the need for an approach that provides an effective solution to the risks countries face and which is robust against planning to avoid or reduce its application or effect. At the same time, this is balanced by the need for an approach to be reasonably straightforward for groups and tax authorities to apply. A short outline of the best practice approach is set out below. Detail on each element of the approach is included in later chapters.

Figure 1.1 Overview of the best practice approach

***De minimis* monetary threshold to remove low risk entities**
Optional
Based on net interest expense of local group

\+

Fixed ratio rule
Allows an entity to deduct net interest expense up to a benchmark net interest/EBITDA ratio
Relevant factors help a country set its benchmark ratio within a corridor of 10%-30%

\+

Group ratio rule
Allows an entity to deduct net interest expense up to its group's net interest/EBITDA ratio, where this is higher than the benchmark fixed ratio
Option for a country to apply an uplift to a group's net third party interest expense of up to 10%

Option for a country to apply a different group ratio rule or no group ratio rule

\+

Carry forward of disallowed interest /unused interest capacity and/or carry back of disallowed interest
Optional

\+

Targeted rules to support general interest limitation rules and address specific risks

\+

Specific rules to address issues raised by the banking and insurance sectors

23. The best practice approach is based around a fixed ratio rule which limits an entity's net interest deductions to a fixed percentage of its profit, measured using earnings before interest, taxes, depreciation and amortisation (EBITDA) based on tax numbers. This is a straightforward rule to apply and ensures that an entity's interest deductions are directly linked to its economic activity. It also directly links these deductions to an

entity's taxable income, which makes the rule reasonably robust against planning. As described in Chapter 5, although EBITDA is the recommended measure of earnings to be used, the best practice allows a country the flexibility to introduce rules based on earnings before interest and taxes (EBIT). In limited cases, a country may apply a fixed ratio rule based on asset values rather than earnings. Chapter 6 includes factors which a country should take into account in setting the benchmark ratio for a fixed ratio rule, within a corridor of 10% to 30%.

24. A fixed ratio rule provides a country with a level of protection against base erosion and profit shifting, but it is a blunt tool which does not take into account the fact that groups operating in different sectors may require different amounts of leverage, and even within a sector some groups are more highly leveraged for non-tax reasons. If a benchmark fixed ratio is set at a level appropriate to tackle base erosion and profit shifting, it could lead to double taxation for groups which are leveraged above this level. Therefore, countries are encouraged to combine a robust and effective fixed ratio rule with a group ratio rule which allows an entity to deduct more interest expense in certain circumstances. A group ratio rule may be introduced as a separate provision from the fixed ratio rule, or as an integral part of an overall rule including both fixed ratio and group ratio tests.

25. Chapter 7 includes a description of a group ratio rule, which allows an entity that exceeds the benchmark fixed ratio to deduct interest expense up to the net third party interest/EBITDA ratio of its group, where this is higher. In calculating the group's ratio, a country may also apply an uplift of up to 10% to the group's net third party interest expense (i.e. its third party interest expense after deducting third party interest income). Under this approach, only net interest expense which takes an entity's net interest/EBITDA ratio above the higher of the benchmark fixed ratio and the group's ratio is disallowed. This rule should complement the fixed ratio rule and provide a robust response to base erosion and profit shifting involving interest expense. However, countries may also apply different group ratio rules, including those using asset-based ratios, so long as these rules only permit an entity to exceed the benchmark fixed ratio where it is able to demonstrate that a relevant financial ratio is in line with that of its group. A country may also decide to apply a fixed ratio rule in isolation. Where a country does not apply a group ratio rule, it should apply the fixed ratio rule consistently to entities in multinational and domestic groups, without improper discrimination. In all cases, under the best practice approach a country should implement the fixed ratio rule using a benchmark ratio which is sufficiently low to address base erosion and profit shifting.

26. In order to remove entities which pose the lowest risk from the scope of a general interest limitation rule, a country may apply a *de minimis* threshold based on a monetary value of net interest expense. Entities falling below this threshold may deduct interest expense without restriction. Where a group has more than one entity in a country, the threshold should take into account the total net interest expense of the entire local group, including all entities in that country. Where a rule is applied at the level of an individual entity, a country should consider including anti-fragmentation rules to prevent a group avoiding the application of an interest limitation rule by establishing a number of entities, each of which falls below the threshold.

27. Rules which link interest deductions to EBITDA raise issues where an entity's interest expense and earnings arise in different periods. This may be the result of volatility in earnings which means the ability of an entity to deduct interest changes from

year to year, or because an entity has incurred interest expense to fund an investment which will give rise to earnings in a later period. To reduce the effect of these issues, a country may permit entities to carry forward disallowed interest expense or unused interest capacity for use in future periods, or carry back disallowed interest expense into earlier periods. It is suggested countries consider imposing limits on these carry forwards and carry backs.

28. A fixed ratio rule and group ratio rule should provide an effective framework to tackle most base erosion and profit shifting involving interest and payments economically equivalent to interest. These general interest limitation rules should be supplemented by targeted rules, which protect the integrity of the general interest limitation rules and deal with specific base erosion and profit shifting risks which remain.

29. Particular features of the banking and insurance industries mean that the fixed ratio rule and the group ratio rule set out in this report are unlikely to be effective in addressing base erosion and profit shifting involving interest in these sectors. As discussed in Chapter 10, further work will be conducted, to be completed in 2016, to identify targeted rules to deal with the base erosion and profit shifting risks posed by banks and insurance companies.

30. It is recommended that, as a minimum, the best practice approach in this report should apply to all entities that are part of a multinational group. Countries may also apply the best practice approach more broadly to include entities in a domestic group and/or standalone entities which are not part of a group. In certain cases countries may be required to do so. In this regard, Annex A includes a summary of EU law issues, including factors that should be taken into account by EU Member States.

31. The best practice approach set out in this report should provide an effective solution to base erosion and profit shifting involving interest and payments economically equivalent to interest. However, countries are free to apply stricter rules than those set out in this report either for the purposes of combating base erosion and profit shifting or to achieve other tax policy goals. For example, the best practice approach may be supplemented by additional general or targeted interest limitation rules which a country has identified as appropriate to address the risks it faces. It is also recognised that a country may have interest limitation rules that carry out broader policy aims, such as reducing the tax bias in favour of debt finance, and that it will want to retain these, or a country may introduce rules to achieve such aims. An illustration of how the best practice approach may be combined with other interest limitation rules is included as Example 2 in Annex D. Finally, when implementing a best practice approach, each country will need to take into account any obligations under its constitution (such as the equal treatment of taxpayers), as well as the specific features of its overall tax system. This may impact, for example, the application of a *de minimis* threshold, the operation of a fixed ratio rule and group ratio rule, and the use of carry forwards. How the fixed ratio rule and group ratio rule may be applied by countries with separate entity taxation or group taxation systems is considered in Chapter 11.

32. The remainder of this report discusses the structure and operation of the best practice approach in more detail, focusing on the following aspects:

- interest and payments economically equivalent to interest
- who a best practice approach should apply to
- applying a best practice approach based on the level of interest expense or debt

- measuring economic activity using earnings or asset values
- a fixed ratio rule
- a group ratio rule
- addressing volatility and double taxation
- targeted rules
- applying the best practice approach to banking and insurance groups
- implementing the best practice approach.

Chapter 2

Interest and payments economically equivalent to interest

33. Interest cost is treated as a tax deductible expense in most countries, but each country applies its own approach to determine what expenses are treated as interest and therefore deductible for tax purposes. It is not the aim of this report to recommend a definition of interest that is applied by all countries for all tax purposes. Differences will continue to exist between countries as to the items treated as deductible interest expense and countries will continue to use their own definitions of interest for other tax purposes, such as for withholding taxes. However, in identifying best practices for the design of rules to address base erosion and profit shifting, there are benefits in countries taking a broadly consistent approach to the items that should be covered by such rules, improving certainty for business and ensuring a coherent approach to tackling the issue across countries. This chapter therefore sets out the items which should be the subject of a best practice rule to tackle base erosion and profit shifting.

34. At its simplest, interest is the cost of borrowing money. However, if a rule restricted its focus to such a narrow band of payments,[1] it would raise three broad issues:

- It would fail to address the range of base erosion and profit shifting risks that countries face in relation to interest deductions and similar payments.
- It would reduce fairness by applying a different treatment to groups that are in the same economic position but use different forms of financing arrangements.
- Its effect could be easily avoided by groups re-structuring loans into other forms of financing arrangement.

35. To address these issues, rules to tackle base erosion and profit shifting using interest should apply to interest on all forms of debt as well as to other financial payments that are economically equivalent to interest. Payments that are economically equivalent to interest include those which are linked to the financing of an entity and are determined by applying a fixed or variable percentage to an actual or notional principal over time. A rule should also apply to other expenses incurred in connection with the raising of finance, including arrangement fees and guarantee fees. This chapter includes a non-exhaustive list of examples of the types of payment that should be covered by a rule, but it is left to each country to determine how this should be reflected within its domestic law, taking into account existing definitions of interest and other payments. In deciding whether a payment is economically equivalent to interest, the focus should be on its economic substance rather than its legal form.

36. A best practice rule to address base erosion and profit shifting using interest expense should therefore apply to: (i) interest on all forms of debt; (ii) payments economically equivalent to interest; and (iii) expenses incurred in connection with the raising of finance. These should include, but not be restricted to, the following:

- payments under profit participating loans
- imputed interest on instruments such as convertible bonds and zero coupon bonds
- amounts under alternative financing arrangements, such as Islamic finance
- the finance cost element of finance lease payments
- capitalised interest included in the balance sheet value of a related asset, or the amortisation of capitalised interest
- amounts measured by reference to a funding return under transfer pricing rules, where applicable
- notional interest amounts under derivative instruments or hedging arrangements related to an entity's borrowings
- certain foreign exchange gains and losses on borrowings and instruments connected with the raising of finance
- guarantee fees with respect to financing arrangements
- arrangement fees and similar costs related to the borrowing of funds.

37. It is recognised that foreign exchange gains and losses on instruments to hedge or take on a currency exposure connected with the raising of finance are not generally economically equivalent to interest. A country may however wish to treat some or all foreign exchange gains and losses on these instruments as economically equivalent to interest, in line with local tax rules and to reflect the economics of the currency exposure.

38. Throughout this report, references to interest should also be taken to include amounts economically equivalent to interest, unless the context clearly requires otherwise. Similarly, where the report refers to a group's or entity's interest income, this includes receipts of amounts economically equivalent to interest based on the definition and examples in this chapter.

39. The best practice approach does not apply to payments which are not interest, economically equivalent to interest or incurred in connection with the raising of finance. Therefore in general, the rules set out in this report should not limit deductions for items such as:

- foreign exchange gains and losses on monetary items which are not connected with the raising of finance
- amounts under derivative instruments or hedging arrangements which are not related to borrowings, for example commodity derivatives
- discounts on provisions not related to borrowings
- operating lease payments
- royalties
- accrued interest with respect to a defined benefit pension plan.

40. However, any payment (including those listed above) may be subject to limitation under the best practice approach where they are used as part of an arrangement which, taken as a whole, gives rise to amounts which are economically equivalent to interest.

41. An illustration of how this definition could be applied in practice is included as Example 3 in Annex D.

42. Where a country has a rule which grants a deemed deduction by applying a specified percentage to the equity capital of an entity, these deemed deductions are not treated as being interest or a payment economically equivalent to interest for the purposes of this report. These rules and rules having similar effect should be considered further by the OECD in separate work.

Notes

1. Throughout this report, references to payments also include accruals of income or expense.

Chapter 3

Who a best practice approach should apply to

43. Base erosion and profit shifting arise in a range of scenarios, including within a group, with related parties outside a group and through the use of structured arrangements with third parties.[1] The best practice approach addresses the risks posed by each of these scenarios, although different rules may be used to address different types of risk. For the purposes of considering which entities these rules should apply to, entities have been categorised into three types: entities which are part of a multinational group; entities which are part of a domestic group; and standalone entities which are not part of a group. It is recommended that, as a minimum, the best practice approach in this report should apply to all entities that are part of a multinational group. Countries may also apply the best practice approach more broadly to include entities in a domestic group and/or standalone entities which are not part of a group.[2]

Entities which are part of a multinational group

44. As set out in the BEPS Action Plan (OECD, 2013), the deductibility of interest can raise base erosion and profit shifting concerns in both inbound and outbound investment scenarios. Therefore, it is recommended that as a minimum a fixed ratio rule as described in Chapter 6 should apply to all entities which are part of a multinational group.

45. An entity is part of a group if the entity is directly or indirectly controlled by a company, or the entity is a company which directly or indirectly controls one or more other entities. A group is a multinational group where it operates in more than one jurisdiction, including through a permanent establishment.

46. Where a country applies a group ratio rule alongside the fixed ratio rule, it may wish to use a consistent definition between both rules to reduce the risk that an entity subject to the fixed ratio rule is unable to apply the group ratio rule. In this case, the country may instead determine that an entity is part of a group where: (i) the entity is included on a line-by-line basis in the consolidated financial statements of any company; or (ii) the entity would be included on a line-by-line basis in the consolidated financial statements of any company, if that company prepared consolidated financial statements in accordance with any of the accounting standards accepted by the country in applying the group ratio rule (as described in Chapter 7).

47. Where a group has more than one entity in a particular country, the country may apply the fixed ratio rule and group ratio rule to the position of each entity separately, or to the overall position of all group entities in the same country (i.e. the local group).[3] Applying a rule to the overall position of the local group would avoid the scenario where a highly leveraged entity incurs an interest disallowance even though the interest expense of the local group as a whole falls within the limit permitted.

48. If the benchmark fixed ratio is set at an appropriate level, a fixed ratio rule should to a large extent address base erosion and profit shifting concerns involving payments by entities which are part of a multinational group. To ensure the fixed ratio rule is effective in tackling base erosion and profit shifting, it is recommended that all entities which are subject to the fixed ratio rule are also subject to targeted provisions which address planning to reduce the impact of the rule. However, there may be specific risks which are not dealt with by the fixed ratio rule and it is recommended that countries consider introducing targeted rules to deal with these risks. The role of targeted rules within the best practice is discussed in Chapter 9.

Entities which are part of a domestic group

49. Entities in multinational groups pose the main base erosion and profit shifting risk. Therefore, it may be appropriate for a country to restrict the application of a fixed ratio rule to these entities. However, a country may choose to apply a fixed ratio rule more broadly, to include entities in domestic groups (i.e. groups which operate wholly within a single country). This may be part of a broad approach to tackle base erosion and profit shifting in all types of entity, or may be in order to meet other policy goals, such as to avoid competition issues between domestic and multinational groups, to reduce the general tax bias in favour of funding with debt over equity, or to comply with constitutional obligations for the equal treatment of taxpayers. In particular, countries which are EU Member States would need to take into account EU law considerations in designing their domestic rules, to ensure they are compliant with EU law.

50. Where a country applies a fixed ratio rule and a group ratio rule to entities which are part of a domestic group, it may apply the rules either to each entity individually or to the overall position of the domestic group. In either case, the fixed ratio rule should to a large extent address base erosion and profit shifting concerns involving interest. However, there may be specific risks which are not dealt with by the fixed ratio rule and it is recommended that countries consider introducing targeted rules, discussed in Chapter 9, to address these risks.

51. Where a country does not apply a fixed ratio rule to entities in a domestic group, it will be exposed to base erosion and profit shifting risks, in particular involving interest paid to related parties and third parties under structured arrangements. In this case, a country should consider addressing these risks using targeted rules as described in Chapter 9.

Standalone entities which are not part of a group

52. A standalone entity is any entity which is not part of a group. The fact that a standalone entity is not part of any group means that the nature and level of base erosion and profit shifting risk that a standalone entity poses is often different to that posed by entities in a group. In many cases standalone entities are small entities, owned directly by an individual, where there are no other entities under common control. In these cases, due to the entity's small size and lack of related parties, the risk of base erosion and profit shifting involving interest is likely to be relatively low. However, in other cases, standalone entities may be large entities held under complex holding structures involving trusts or partnerships, where there are a number of entities under the control of the same investors. In these cases the level of base erosion and profit shifting risk may be similar to that posed by a group structure. In both scenarios, where base erosion and profit shifting

involving interest does occur, it will arise as a result of payments to related parties and third parties.

53. A country should apply rules to address base erosion and profit shifting risks posed by standalone entities. A country may apply the fixed ratio rule to standalone entities or, recognising the differences between the risks posed by entities in groups and standalone entities, it may tackle risks posed by standalone entities using different rules. In either case, standalone entities should be subject to targeted rules to address specific risks, discussed in Chapter 9. EU Member States would need to take into account EU law considerations in designing their domestic rules, to ensure they are compliant with EU law. Such considerations should be taken into account when designing domestic rules in order to limit their possible negative impact on situations not involving base erosion or profit shifting.

De minimis threshold

54. While the main policy goal of the best practice approach set out in this report is to address base erosion and profit shifting using interest, it is recognised that certain entities may pose a sufficiently low risk that excluding them from a fixed ratio rule and group ratio rule would be appropriate. Excluding these entities from the fixed ratio rule and group ratio rule would mean that a best practice approach can focus on entities which pose material base erosion and profit shifting risk, reducing compliance costs for other entities. Reducing the number of entities covered would also reduce the costs of administering a rule and would allow a tax authority to focus its resources on entities which pose the greatest risk.

55. Countries may therefore introduce a *de minimis* threshold to exclude low risk entities from the scope of the fixed ratio rule and group ratio rule. It is recommended that such a threshold should be based on the total net interest expense of all entities in the local group. Where a country wishes to apply a threshold based on the net interest expense of each entity separately, it is important that these rules are not abused. Therefore, a country should consider introducing anti-fragmentation rules to prevent a group avoiding an interest limitation rule by establishing multiple entities, each of which falls below the threshold.

56. A *de minimis* threshold based on net interest expense should be relatively simple to apply and would ensure that highly-leveraged entities are required to apply a general interest limitation rule regardless of their size. A country should set the level of a *de minimis* threshold to reflect a number of factors, including the local economic and interest rate environment, as well as relevant tax or legal considerations. This may be reviewed and updated periodically to reflect changes in these factors.

Notes

1. The terms "related party" and "structured arrangement" are defined in Chapter 9.
2. There may be cases where a country is required to apply the fixed ratio rule more broadly, for example to entities in domestic groups. For instance, countries may need to take into account any constitutional issues which could have a direct impact on interest limitation rules. In addition, Annex A includes a summary of EU law issues, including factors that should be taken into account by EU Member States.
3. Chapter 11 includes a summary of different approaches that a country may use in applying a fixed ratio rule to a local group, depending upon the structure of its tax system.

Bibliography

OECD (2013), *Action Plan on Base Erosion and Profit Shifting*, OECD Publishing, Paris, http://dx.doi.org/10.1787/9789264202719-en.

Chapter 4

Applying a best practice approach based on the level of interest expense or debt

57. A key cause of base erosion and profit shifting is the ability of a group to artificially separate taxable income from the underlying activities that drive value creation. Therefore, one of the aims of the best practice approach set out in this report is to link the amount of interest deductions in an entity to the level of its taxable economic activity.

Applying the best practice approach to limit the level of interest expense or debt in an entity

58. A general interest limitation rule may operate directly, by restricting the amount of interest an entity may deduct for tax purposes, or indirectly, by restricting the amount of debt with respect to which an entity may claim deductions for interest. In considering which approach to include in the best practice recommendation, a number of factors have been taken into account. These include the following:

- Base erosion and profit shifting using interest is driven by the level of tax deductible expense incurred by an entity. A rule which directly limits the level of interest deductions an entity may claim addresses this.
- A rule which limits the level of debt in an entity will not necessarily address base erosion and profit shifting risks where an excessive rate of interest is applied to a loan. Therefore, such a rule would need to have a further mechanism to identify the maximum interest on the permitted level of debt. This could be done by applying an arm's length test or apportioning an entity's actual interest expense, but these approaches add a step to the operation of a rule and increase complexity.
- A best practice approach should apply to base erosion and profit shifting involving interest and payments economically equivalent to interest. However, for some payments economically equivalent to interest, there may be no existing requirement for an entity to separately recognise a debt linked to the payment. It should therefore be easier for entities and tax authorities to identify and value the payments of interest (and economically equivalent payments) for which tax relief is being claimed.
- The level of debt in an entity may vary throughout a period, which means that the amount of debt on a particular date, or even an average for the period, may not be representative of an entity's true position. On the other hand, the level of interest expense in an entity will reflect all changes in borrowings throughout the period. This is therefore likely to give a more accurate picture of the entity's actual position over the period.

- A rule based on the level of debt in an entity could take into account the fact that two entities with the same amount of debt may for commercial reasons be subject to different rates of interest (e.g. taking into account the currency of borrowings and credit risk). This could also be done under a rule that directly limits an entity's interest expense (e.g. by taking a group's actual level of interest expense into account).
- The level of debt in an entity is under the control of the entity's management and so is generally predictable. The amount of interest expense, however, may vary reflecting changes in interest rates. This means that a rule that directly limits the level of interest expense could make it difficult for an entity to enter into long-term borrowings if there is a risk that interest rates could increase and it would suffer an interest disallowance in future periods.

59. Taking these factors into account, and given the key policy objective is to tackle base erosion and profit shifting involving interest and payments economically equivalent to interest, the best practice set out in this report includes rules which directly limit the level of interest expense that an entity may deduct for tax purposes. It also includes features, such as the group ratio rule, which should address some of the possible issues this raises. For example, if a group represents a greater credit risk and is required to pay a higher rate of interest on its third party debt, a group ratio rule will take this into account in setting a limit on tax deductions for entities within the group. As set out in the Introduction, a country may continue to apply an arm's length test alongside the best practice approach. For example, this could ensure that the amount of interest expense claimed by an entity is in accordance with the arm's length principle, but this amount is then subject to limitation under the best practice approach in this report.

Applying the best practice approach to limit an entity's gross interest expense or net interest expense

60. Another key question is whether a general interest limitation rule should apply to the interest an entity incurs on its borrowings without any offset for interest income (gross interest expense) or after offsetting the interest income it receives (net interest expense).

61. A gross interest rule has the benefit of simplicity and is also likely to be more difficult for groups to avoid through planning. However, a gross interest rule could lead to double taxation where each entity is subject to tax on its full gross interest income, but part of its gross interest expense is disallowed.

62. A net interest rule would reduce the risk of double taxation, as an entity's interest income would be set against its interest expense before the interest limitation is applied. It would also allow an entity to raise third party debt and on-lend borrowed funds within its group, without the entity incurring a disallowance of part of its gross interest expense. Taking into account these considerations, the general interest limitation rules contained in this report apply to an entity's net interest expense paid to third parties, related parties and intragroup, after offsetting interest income.[1] Rules should apply to all of an entity's net interest expense, as discussed in Chapter 2, to ensure that a broad range of base erosion and profit shifting risks are addressed, including where excessive third party interest expense is incurred in a high tax country.

63. However, the fact that an entity has a relatively low net interest expense does not mean that base erosion and profit shifting is not taking place. For example, an entity with

net interest income could use interest expense to shelter this income from tax. An entity may also disguise other forms of taxable income as interest income, reducing the level of net interest expense to which the rule can apply. Therefore, it is recommended that countries supplement the general interest limitation rules with targeted provisions which disallow gross interest expense in specific situations identified as posing base erosion and profit shifting risk. This is discussed in Chapter 9. Rules which apply to limit an entity's net interest expense will also have no impact on entities which, because of their business model, are typically receivers of net interest income. This arises in particular in the banking and insurance sectors, which are discussed in Chapter 10.

An option to exclude certain public-benefit projects

64. The best practice approach set out in this report places a general limit on the level of net interest expense that an entity may deduct for tax purposes. The fixed ratio rule should be applied consistently to all interest paid to third parties, related parties and group entities. However, as an exception to this general principle, a country may choose to exclude interest expense incurred on specific third party loans meeting the conditions set out below from the scope of the fixed ratio rule and group ratio rule. Except as set out in this report, other exclusions should not be applied.

65. In some countries, privately-owned public-benefit assets may be large-scale assets financed using a high proportion of debt. However, because of the nature of the assets and the close connection with the public sector, some such financing arrangements present little or no base erosion or profit shifting risk.

66. Taking account of the specific circumstances of the public sector, a country may exclude certain amounts with respect to third party loans linked to specific assets when calculating an entity's net interest expense which is subject to limitation under the best practice approach. To ensure this approach is tightly targeted only on those projects which do not pose a base erosion or profit shifting risk, the following conditions must be met:

- An entity (the operator) establishes a project to provide (or upgrade), operate and/or maintain assets on a long-term basis, lasting not less than 10 years, and these assets cannot be disposed of at the discretion of the operator.
- A public sector body or a public benefit entity (the grantor),[2] contractually or otherwise obliges the operator to provide goods or services in which there is a general public interest.[3] This provision must be subject to specific controls or a regulatory framework in addition to rules applying generally to companies or other commercial entities within a jurisdiction.
- Interest is payable by the operator on a loan or loans obtained from and owed to third party lenders on non-recourse terms, so that the lender only has recourse to and a charge over the assets and income streams of the specific project. Arrangements involving recourse to other assets, guarantees from other group companies or which otherwise seek to offer recourse beyond the project assets would not qualify for the exclusion.
- The loan or loans made to the operator do not exceed the value or estimated value of the assets at acquisition or once constructed, unless additional investment is made to maintain or increase their value. Subject to minimal and incidental

lending to a third party (such as a bank deposit), none of the funds should be on-lent.

- The operator, the interest expense, the project assets and income arising from the project are all in the same country, where the income must be subject to tax at ordinary rates.[4] Where the project assets are held in a permanent establishment, the exclusion will only apply to the extent that income arising from the project is subject to tax at ordinary rates in the country applying the exclusion.
- Similar projects of the operator or similar projects of other entities of the operator´s group are not substantially less leveraged with third-party-debt, taking into account project maturities.

67. Countries making use of the exclusion may impose additional rules before allowing an exclusion to apply, in order to prevent the exclusion being used by businesses not engaged in projects which deliver public benefits. These might include a requirement that obtaining the exclusion is not a main purpose of structuring the financing arrangements to meet the other conditions of the exclusion. Countries making use of the exclusion should publish full information about the scope of domestic legislation and the circumstances in which it can be used, and should also introduce mechanisms to provide for spontaneous exchange of information relating to the entities benefiting from the exclusion and investors in these with all relevant jurisdictions. The framework in Chapter 5 of the OECD Report *Countering Harmful Tax Practices More Effectively, Taking into Account Transparency and Substance* (OECD, 2015) would be used to determine the jurisdictions with which to spontaneously exchange such information. Countries adopting the exclusion should monitor its operation with a view to assisting in the review referred to below. Such countries should require taxpayers to clearly disclose any use of this exclusion.

68. Where this exclusion applies, a country applying the exclusion should also take steps to ensure that the project earnings and assets, and related interest expense, are not used to permit further interest deductions for the entity or other group entities in the country. Therefore, the country should adjust the operation of the fixed ratio rule and group ratio rule, so that where an entity benefits from this exclusion:

- Any earnings arising from the project (and/or the project assets) are excluded from the calculation of earnings or asset values under the fixed ratio rule and group ratio rule.
- The interest expense which has been excluded from limitation should not be included in the group's net third party interest expense when applying the group ratio rule.

69. There is also a risk that interest which benefits from this exclusion will be used to increase the level of net interest deductions for group entities in other countries in which a group ratio rule is applied. Therefore, in applying the group ratio rule, a country may exclude any third party interest expense which benefits from an exclusion in any other country. Similarly, project earnings and assets may be excluded from the calculation of group earnings or asset values. Countries may obtain information on whether the exclusion has been applied using the exchange of information provisions contained in applicable international agreements. A country may also choose not to require the adjustments in this paragraph, in order to minimise complexity.

70. The design and operation of this exclusion will be included in the initial review of the best practice, to be conducted by no later than the end of 2020. This will include consideration of how the exclusion is being used, to ensure it is not giving rise to base erosion or profit shifting risks. Following this review, the exclusion may be revised or removed.

71. EU law issues are considered in Annex A.

Notes

1. The term "related party" is defined in Chapter 9.
2. A public benefit entity will typically be an entity whose primary objective is to provide goods or services for the general public, community or social benefit and where any equity is provided with a view to supporting the entity's primary objectives rather than to provide a financial return to equity holders. The definition of a public benefit entity used by a country may be contained in law or a relevant applicable accounting standard.
3. Assets that provide goods and services in which there is a general public interest would generally refer to assets that are public goods.
4. Countries which are Member States of the European Union would need to take into account EU law considerations in designing their domestic rules.

Bibliography

OECD (2015), *Countering Harmful Tax Practices More Effectively, Taking into Account Transparency and Substance, Action 5 - 2015 Final Report*, OECD/G20 Base Erosion and Profit Shifting Project, OECD Publishing, Paris, http://dx.doi.org/10.1787/9789264241190-en.

Chapter 5

Measuring economic activity using earnings or asset values

72. Fixed ratio rules and group ratio rules restrict the ability of an entity to deduct interest expense based on an objective measure of its economic activity. Work to develop a best practice approach has focused on earnings and asset values, as the measures which most clearly reflect the level of activity and value creation within a multinational group.

Measuring economic activity using earnings

73. As highlighted in the previous chapter, a goal of the BEPS project is to address practices that artificially separate taxable income from the activities that generate it. For most entities it is expected that there should be a clear correlation between earnings and taxable income. Therefore, measuring economic activity using earnings should be the most effective way to ensure that the ability to deduct net interest expense is matched with the activities that generate taxable income and drive value creation. In addition, depending upon the definition of earnings used, this is a useful indicator of an entity's ability to meet its obligations to pay interest, and therefore is one of the key factors used in determining the amount of debt an entity is able to borrow.

74. Another benefit of an earnings-based approach is that it makes a general interest limitation rule more robust against planning. Where the level of deductible interest expense in an entity is linked to earnings, a group can only increase net interest deductions in a particular country by increasing earnings in that country. Similarly, any restructuring to move profits out of a country will also reduce net interest deductions in the country. On the assumption that an increase in earnings will also give rise to an increase in taxable income, it is unlikely that the level of earnings will be manipulated in order to increase the interest deductions in a country.

75. The BEPS Action Plan (OECD, 2013) specifically requires the development of rules to address base erosion and profit shifting using interest expense to fund tax exempt or tax deferred income. A third important benefit of an approach using earnings is that the definition of earnings can be adapted to exclude income which is subject to favourable tax treatment. An obvious example would be dividend income, which in many countries is exempt from tax or is taxed at a reduced rate (subject to conditions such as a minimum holding requirement).

76. The main disadvantage of earnings as a measure of economic activity is that an entity's earnings may be relatively volatile and there is a limit to the extent this can be controlled by a group. This means that under an earnings-based rule it may be hard for an entity to anticipate the level of net interest expense that will be permitted from year to year. This could make it difficult for an entity to calculate a cost of debt for long term projects, without knowing the extent to which its interest cost will be deductible. To an extent, these issues may be addressed in the design of a best practice approach, for example by allowing an entity to measure economic activity using the average earnings over a number of periods or

by permitting an entity to carry forward disallowed interest expense and unused capacity to deduct interest. These approaches are discussed in Chapter 8.

77. A particular aspect of earnings volatility is the possibility that an entity may be in a negative earnings (i.e. loss-making) position. Under an earnings-based approach, an entity with negative earnings will be unable to deduct its net interest expense in the current period. In principle, this could mean that an entity with losses could be required to pay taxes as a result of an interest disallowance. However, this risk could be reduced depending upon the definition of earnings used, and whether this is based on tax or accounting information. Other mechanisms, such as the carry forward of disallowed interest expense, should enable a loss-making entity to retain the benefit of interest deductions and claim relief once it returns to profit.

Definition of earnings

78. In terms of the definition of earnings to be used, earnings before interest, taxes, depreciation and amortisation (EBITDA) and earnings before interest and taxes (EBIT) are both possible options. In either, non-taxable income such as branch profits or dividend income that benefit from a participation exemption should not be included in the calculation of earnings. Appropriate adjustments should also be made for taxable branch profits and dividend income to the extent that they are shielded from tax by foreign tax credits, in order to address the base erosion and profit shifting issues which are the subject of this report.[1] EBITDA is the most common measure of earnings currently used by countries with earnings-based tests. By excluding the two major non-cash costs in a typical income statement (depreciation of fixed assets and amortisation of intangible assets), EBITDA is a guide to the ability of an entity to meet its obligations to pay interest. It is also a measure of earnings which is often used by lenders in deciding how much interest expense an entity can reasonably afford to bear. On the other hand, using EBITDA potentially favours entities operating in sectors with high levels of fixed asset investment. This is because EBITDA does not include the write-down of capitalised costs such as investment in plant and machinery, whereas it does take into account revenue costs which are the majority of the cost base for entities in other sectors. Data suggests that, across all industry sectors, average gross interest/EBIT ratios based on information taken from consolidated financial statements are approximately 40% higher than average gross interest/EBITDA ratios, although there can be significant variation between different industry sectors.

Measuring economic activity using asset values

79. The main benefit of an assets-based approach to measuring economic activity is that in general asset values are typically more stable (except in the case of revaluations and write-downs, and assets which are carried at fair value under accounting rules). This means that using asset values as a basis for measuring economic activity within a group should give rise to a relatively steady and predictable limit on the level of interest relief that can be claimed. This would improve certainty for groups and could also reduce compliance costs. In addition, an approach based on asset values would mean that entities with losses would still be able to deduct an amount of net interest expense, which may not be possible under an earnings-based approach.

80. In order to provide an accurate measure of an entity's economic activity, an assets-based rule should take into account the value of those assets which drive the creation of value for the group. These would include assets such as land and buildings, plant and equipment, intangible assets, and financial assets which give rise to income other than

interest, but excluding assets which give rise to non-taxable income (such as equity holdings which give rise to tax exempt dividends). However, a key issue surrounding an assets-based approach for the purposes of applying a fixed ratio rule is achieving a consistent and acceptable model for valuing each of these classes of assets. In terms of tangible assets, such as land and buildings and plant and equipment, a requirement to use market values of assets would be impractical and impose an excessive compliance burden on groups. However, an amortised historic cost valuation could give rise to inconsistencies depending upon the age of assets and is subject to influence by decisions of management, for instance on depreciation periods and the timing of revaluations and write downs. Historic cost is also unlikely to represent the actual value an asset contributes to a group's economic activity. Intangible assets including trademarks and patents can be a group's most valuable assets. However, accounting standards often impose stringent requirements on groups before they are able to recognise an intangible asset on their balance sheet, particularly where the asset has been internally created. This means that for a number of large groups, an approach to limiting interest deductions based on asset values for accounting purposes will not directly take into account the group's most valuable assets (although intangible assets may be indirectly reflected to the extent they give rise to earnings which are not distributed and so are included in retained earnings within equity). A specific area of difference in the treatment of assets under accounting standards is in the recognition of financial assets including derivative balances, and in particular the ability of groups to report positions on a gross or net basis. This can result in a significant difference in the value of a group's total assets and under some accounting standards is left to the discretion of a group's management, subject to conditions being met. These issues are in particular a problem in applying a fixed ratio rule based on asset values as in these cases a fixed benchmark ratio is applied to asset values which can vary significantly based on the accounting standards and policies applied by different groups. Concerns over the recognition and valuation of assets may be less of an issue in applying a group ratio rule, so long as a consistent approach is taken at entity and group level.

Proposed approach

81. On balance and taking into account the above factors, it appears that for a fixed ratio rule earnings is the most appropriate measure of economic activity, for groups operating in the majority of sectors and in different countries. In applying a group ratio rule, the differences between an earnings-based and an assets-based approach are less significant. This is reflected in the best practice approach set out in this report.

82. It is recommended that a fixed ratio rule should measure earnings using EBITDA. However, a country may apply a fixed ratio rule which measures earnings using EBIT, so long as the other elements of the rule are consistent with the best practice in this report. Where a country applies a fixed ratio rule based on EBIT, the benchmark net interest/EBIT ratio used should be equivalent to the appropriate benchmark net interest/EBITDA ratio described in Chapter 6, taking into account where the particular country would be placed within the corridor based on the factors in that chapter. In considering whether a benchmark net interest/EBIT ratio is equivalent to a net interest/EBITDA ratio, a country should take into account differences between average EBIT and EBITDA figures for the major sectors in its economy.

83. Where the economy of a particular country is highly reliant on heavily capitalised groups whose activities rely on tangible fixed assets with long depreciation periods, earnings should still be a suitable measure of economic activity for the purposes of applying a fixed

ratio rule. However, in this case asset values may exceptionally be used as an acceptable alternative. Where a country applies a fixed ratio rule based on asset values, other elements of the rule should be consistent with the best practice approach. For example, the rule should apply to limit net interest expense payable to third parties and group entities located within the country and in other countries. The assets included in a valuation should include the main categories of assets which drive economic activity in a group but should exclude assets which give rise to non-taxable income such as dividends which qualify for a participation exemption. Asset values may be based on accounting or tax numbers, but this should be applied consistently. The benchmark net interest/assets ratio should be equivalent to the appropriate benchmark net interest/EBITDA ratio described in Chapter 6, taking into account where the particular country would be placed within the corridor based on the factors in that chapter. In considering whether a benchmark net interest/assets ratio is equivalent to a net interest/EBITDA ratio, a country may take into account the number of groups affected and the overall level of net interest expense disallowed.

84. Where a country applies a fixed ratio rule and group ratio rule both based on earnings, it is recommended that either EBITDA or EBIT be used for both rules. As described in Chapter 7, a country may also apply a fixed ratio rule based on earnings alongside a group ratio rule based on asset values, so long as the group ratio rule only permits an entity to exceed the benchmark fixed ratio where it is able to demonstrate that a relevant financial ratio (such as equity/total assets) is in line with that of its group.

Notes

1. Where branch profits benefit from a participation exemption, the entity's EBITDA or EBIT should be reduced by an amount equal to the EBITDA or EBIT of the branch. Where branch profits are taxed, an entity's EBITDA or EBIT should be reduced by an amount equal to part of the branch's EBITDA or EBIT, in proportion to the extent that the tax on branch profits is sheltered by tax credits. For example, under one possible approach, if 25% of the entity's tax liability on the branch profits is sheltered by tax credits, the entity's EBITDA or EBIT should be reduced by an amount equal to 25% of the EBITDA or EBIT of the branch.

Bibliography

OECD (2013), *Action Plan on Base Erosion and Profit Shifting*, OECD Publishing, Paris, http://dx.doi.org/10.1787/9789264202719-en.

Chapter 6

Fixed ratio rule

Aim of a fixed ratio rule

85. The premise underlying the fixed ratio rule is that an entity should be able to deduct interest expense up to a specified proportion of EBITDA, ensuring that a portion of an entity's profit remains subject to tax in a country. A fixed ratio rule can apply to all entities, including those in a multinational group, a domestic group and standalone entities. The underlying benchmark fixed ratio is determined by a country's government and applies irrespective of the actual leverage of an entity or its group. Interest paid to third parties, related parties[1] and group entities is deductible up to this fixed ratio, but any interest which takes the entity's ratio above this benchmark is disallowed.

86. The key advantage of a fixed ratio rule is that it is relatively simple for companies to apply and tax administrations to administer. On the other hand, a fixed ratio rule does not take into account the fact that groups operating in different sectors may require different amounts of leverage, and even within a sector groups may adopt different funding strategies for non-tax reasons. Applying a fixed ratio rule differently to groups in different sectors would inevitably make a rule more complex to administer, in particular where a sector cannot be easily defined or where a group has activities across more than one sector. The option to exclude interest funding certain public-benefit projects described in Chapter 4 may help to address these issues for some entities. However, in general, a country should apply the fixed ratio rule consistently, using the same benchmark fixed ratio, to groups in all sectors (with the exception of groups in the banking and insurance sectors, which are considered in Chapter 10, for which targeted rules are being considered).

87. However, groups in certain sectors may benefit from economic rent that means they are able to generate high levels of EBITDA, which under the general approach described in this report could give rise to relatively high levels of net interest deductions. A country may therefore choose to apply a fixed ratio rule more strictly to groups in these sectors. For example, groups in sectors which benefit from economic rents may be subject to a lower benchmark fixed ratio, or the calculation of entity EBITDA may be adjusted to strip out the effect of the economic rent.

Operation of a fixed ratio rule

88. Fixed ratio rules apply a predetermined benchmark fixed ratio to the earnings of an entity or a local group to calculate the maximum deductible interest expense.[2] Calculating the amount of any interest expense disallowance under a fixed ratio rule involves a three step process: firstly, calculating the appropriate measure of EBITDA; secondly, applying the statutory benchmark fixed ratio to an entity's EBITDA to

determine the maximum deductible interest expense; and thirdly, comparing this with the actual interest expense of the entity. The calculation of EBITDA should be based on values that are determined under the tax rules of the country applying the rule. The use of tax figures to calculate entity EBITDA has a number of advantages. Firstly, the rule should be reasonably straightforward to apply and audit. Secondly, using tax numbers reduces the risk that an entity with negative EBITDA is required to pay taxes as a result of an interest disallowance. Finally, linking interest deductions to taxable earnings means it is more difficult for a group to increase the limit on net interest deductions without also increasing the level of taxable income in a country.

Step 1: Calculating the measure of earnings

89. An entity's EBITDA should be calculated by adding back to its taxable income, the tax values for: (i) net interest expense and net payments equivalent to interest payments as defined in Chapter 2; and (ii) depreciation and amortization. Tax exempt income, such as exempt dividend income or foreign earnings that are tax exempt, should not form part of the entity's EBITDA figure. The rationale behind excluding exempt dividend income is to address concerns related to the outbound investment scenario as described in Action 4.

Step 2: Applying the statutory benchmark fixed ratio to earnings

90. Following the calculation of the entity's EBITDA, the statutory benchmark fixed ratio will be applied to the EBITDA figure. The result determines the maximum amount of interest expense that the entity is allowed to deduct for tax purposes.

Step 3: Comparing maximum deductible interest expense with actual interest expense

91. In the last step, the maximum amount that the entity is allowed to deduct for tax purposes is then compared with the entity's actual net interest expense.

92. Net interest expense in excess of the maximum allowable amount is disallowed. An illustration of how a fixed ratio rule might operate in practice is included as Example 4 in Annex D. This example also illustrates the potential advantages and disadvantages of applying a fixed ratio rule at the level of the local group.

Setting a benchmark fixed ratio

93. An effective fixed ratio rule requires a country to set the benchmark fixed ratio at a level which is appropriate to tackle base erosion and profit shifting. At the same time, it is recognised that countries differ in terms of both their economic environment and the presence of other targeted tax rules which specifically address base erosion and profit shifting risk involving interest. There are many factors which could affect the competitiveness of countries to attract investment, including the tax rate, composition of the tax base and interest deductibility rules. Therefore, without an agreed best practice approach, there is a risk that competitiveness concerns would drive countries to adopt benchmark fixed ratios at a high level which would allow more interest expense to be deducted and reduce the effectiveness of the rule in tackling base erosion and profit shifting.

A corridor of benchmark fixed ratios

94. In order to address base erosion and profit shifting risks, by co-ordinating the approach to setting a benchmark fixed ratio between countries and reduce the risk that countries will be driven to apply a ratio at a level which is too high to address base erosion and profit shifting risks, it is recommended that countries set their benchmark fixed ratio within a best practice range or "corridor".

95. In setting a best practice corridor, the key aim is to identify a range of benchmark fixed ratios which:

- allows the majority of groups to deduct an amount equivalent to their net third party interest expense (assuming net interest expense is spread around the group in accordance with accounting-EBITDA)
- limits the extent to which groups can use intragroup interest expense to claim total net interest deductions in excess of their net third party interest expense.

96. Financial data provided to the OECD by BIAC/PwC[3] illustrates the proportion of publicly traded multinational groups with positive EBITDA that would in principle be able to deduct an amount equivalent to their net third party interest expense, if a benchmark fixed ratio is set at different levels. This assumes that a group's net interest expense is spread around the group in accordance with EBITDA. Groups with negative EBITDA are not included in this analysis, as the impact of a fixed ratio rule on an entity with negative EBITDA is the same irrespective of the level at which a benchmark fixed ratio is set. The numbers below are based on average figures over the period 2009 to 2013:[4]

- At a benchmark fixed ratio of 10%, 62% of these groups would in principle be able to deduct all of their net third party interest expense.
- At a benchmark fixed ratio of 20%, 78% of these groups would in principle be able to deduct all of their net third party interest expense.
- At a benchmark fixed ratio of 30%, 87% of these groups would in principle be able to deduct all of their net third party interest expense.
- At a benchmark fixed ratio of 40%, 91% of these groups would in principle be able to deduct all of their net third party interest expense.
- At a benchmark fixed ratio of 50%, 93% of these groups would in principle be able to deduct all of their net third party interest expense.

97. Once a benchmark fixed ratio exceeds 30%, the rate at which more groups are able to deduct all of their net third party interest expense increases more slowly. However, at this level, a significant proportion of groups may have an incentive to increase the level of intragroup debt in order to claim net interest deductions in excess of their net third party interest expense. For example, based on the financial data referred to in the paragraph above, around half of publicly traded multinational groups with positive EBITDA have a net third party interest/EBITDA ratio of 5% or below. Therefore, at a benchmark fixed ratio of 30%, there is a risk that these groups could deduct up to six times their actual net third party interest, assuming there are no impediments to the use of intragroup debt. This risk increases if a benchmark fixed ratio is set above this level. On the basis of this analysis, and balancing the goals of allowing most groups to deduct their net third party interest expense and limiting the risk that groups will deduct more than this

amount, it is recommended that countries applying a fixed ratio rule based on a net interest/EBITDA ratio set their benchmark fixed ratio within a corridor of 10% to 30%. As set out in Chapter 11, this corridor may be revised following an initial review of the best practice, to be completed by no later than the end of 2020.

98. Within the best practice corridor, a majority of groups with positive EBITDA should in principle be able to deduct all of their net third party interest expense. A country could also include other elements of the best practice approach to enable entities in groups with a net third party interest/EBITDA ratio above the benchmark fixed ratio to deduct more net interest expense, where they pose a low risk of base erosion and profit shifting. For example, a group ratio rule may be used to allow an entity which exceeds the benchmark fixed ratio to deduct more net interest expense up to the level of the group's net third party interest/EBITDA ratio where this is higher. A country may also apply a *de minimis* threshold to exclude from the scope of a fixed ratio rule and group ratio rule entities with low net interest expense.

Factors to assist countries in setting a benchmark fixed ratio

99. It is recommended that countries set their benchmark fixed ratio within the corridor of 10% to 30%. However, it should be recognised that countries differ in terms of their legal framework and economic circumstances and, in setting a benchmark fixed ratio within the corridor which is suitable for tackling base erosion and profit shifting, a country should therefore take into account a number of factors, including the following:

1. A country may apply a higher benchmark fixed ratio if it operates a fixed ratio rule in isolation, rather than operating it in combination with a group ratio rule.
2. A country may apply a higher benchmark fixed ratio if it does not permit the carry forward of unused interest capacity or carry back of disallowed interest expense.
3. A country may apply a higher benchmark fixed ratio if it applies other targeted rules that specifically address the base erosion and profit shifting risks to be dealt with under Action 4.
4. A country may apply a higher benchmark fixed ratio if it has high interest rates compared with those of other countries.
5. A country may apply a higher benchmark fixed ratio, where for constitutional or other legal reasons (e.g. EU law requirements) it has to apply the same treatment to different types of entities which are viewed as legally comparable, even if these entities pose different levels of risk.
6. A country may apply different fixed ratios depending upon the size of an entity's group.

100. These factors are considered in more detail below.

A country may apply a higher benchmark fixed ratio if it operates a fixed ratio rule in isolation, rather than operating it in combination with a group ratio rule

101. Where a country operates a fixed ratio rule alongside a group ratio rule, an entity which exceeds the fixed ratio may be able to deduct more net interest expense up to the relevant financial ratio of its group. The country is therefore able to apply a benchmark fixed ratio at a lower level, relying on the group ratio rule to moderate the impact of this on entities in groups which are highly leveraged. On the other hand, where a country

introduces a fixed ratio rule without a group ratio rule, it may apply a higher benchmark fixed ratio.

A country may apply a higher benchmark fixed ratio if it does not permit the carry forward of unused interest capacity or carry back of disallowed interest expense

102. Unused interest capacity is the amount by which an entity's net interest expense is below the maximum amount permitted under the fixed ratio rule. As discussed in Chapter 8, where a country permits unused interest capacity to be carried forward, this could give rise to a tax asset which may be monetised by increasing the entity's net interest expense or by reducing its EBITDA. As these behaviours should not be encouraged by a rule to tackle base erosion and profit shifting, a country which allows the carry forward of unused interest capacity should apply a lower benchmark fixed ratio to reduce this incentive. Similarly, a country which permits the carry back of disallowed interest expense, which gives rise to the same risk, should also apply a lower benchmark fixed ratio. The weight which should be attached to this factor would depend upon the extent to which a country incorporates the restrictions discussed in Chapter 8. A country which does not allow either a carry forward of unused interest capacity or a carry back of disallowed interest expense may apply a higher benchmark fixed ratio.

A country may apply a higher benchmark fixed ratio if it applies other targeted rules that specifically address the base erosion and profit shifting risks to be dealt with under Action 4

103. Action 4 focuses on the development of best practices in the design of rules to prevent base erosion and profit shifting through the use of third party, related party and intragroup interest, including payments economically equivalent to interest, to achieve excessive interest deductions or finance the production of exempt or deferred income. The recommended best practice approach includes the fixed ratio rule described in this chapter, but it is recognised that other targeted interest limitation rules may also be effective in tackling some of these risks. For example, a country may have a targeted rule which disallows all interest expense used to fund tax exempt income. Where a country has targeted rules which specifically address the base erosion and profit shifting risks to be dealt with under Action 4, and it applies these rules in practice, these may reduce pressure on the fixed ratio rule meaning that a higher benchmark fixed ratio could be applied. The extent to which this factor supports a higher benchmark fixed ratio depends upon the extent to which the specific base erosion and profit shifting risks involving interest and targeted by Action 4 are addressed. Where a country does not have other rules which specifically deal with the base erosion and profit shifting risks targeted by Action 4, it should apply a lower benchmark fixed ratio.

A country may apply a higher benchmark fixed ratio if it has high interest rates compared with those of other countries

104. The net interest/EBITDA ratio of entities which raise third party debt locally can be impacted by a number of factors, including the level of a country's interest rates. Where a country's interest rates are high relative to those in other countries, the country may recognise this by applying a higher benchmark fixed ratio. This is not intended to favour entities operating in a high interest rate country, but simply recognises the fact that these entities are likely to be subject to a higher cost of funds. The extent to which this factor supports a higher benchmark fixed ratio depends upon the extent to which interest

rates are higher than those in other countries. However, a country with high interest rates may still apply a low benchmark fixed ratio. For example, where a country applies the same benchmark fixed ratio to all entities, including those in large groups which are less likely to be exposed to differences in interest rates between countries, it may decide that it is not appropriate for its high interest rate to be taken into account when setting the ratio. Where a country has low interest rates compared with other countries, it should apply a lower benchmark fixed ratio. In comparing its interest rates with those of other countries, a country may take into account one or more relevant rates, such as the central bank rate, the long-term government bond rate and the average corporate bond rate for entities with a good credit rating (for example, equivalent to a credit rating of "A" or above). Whether a particular interest rate is high or low must be judged in comparison with other countries and will change over time as interest rates move. Currently, it is suggested that a long-term government bond rate that is above 5% may be considered to be high.

A country may apply a higher benchmark fixed ratio, where for constitutional or other legal reasons (e.g. EU law requirements) it has to apply the same treatment to different types of entities which are viewed as legally comparable, even if these entities pose different levels of risk

105. As set out in Chapter 3, the main base erosion and profit risk involving interest is posed by entities in multinational groups. Therefore, within the best practice approach, a country may restrict the application of the fixed ratio rule to these entities. However, in some cases, constitutional or legal requirements mean that a country is also required to apply the fixed ratio rule to other entities which are seen as legally comparable, including entities in domestic groups and/or standalone entities which may pose less risk of base erosion and profit shifting involving interest. In this case, because the country is required to apply the same treatment to entities which are legally comparable, including those which pose less base erosion and profit shifting risk, the country may apply a benchmark fixed ratio at a higher level within the corridor. In such situations, a country may alternatively decide to apply a lower ratio in order to ensure that base erosion and profit shifting involving interest is addressed, even though this would also be applied to entities which pose less risk.

A country may apply different fixed ratios depending upon the size of an entity's group

106. In general, entities in large groups are in a different position to other entities when raising third party debt. For example, large groups are more likely to raise third party debt centrally, they may have better access to global capital markets, and they may have greater bargaining power with lenders. Large groups also often have sophisticated treasury functions to manage the financial position of the group, including its interest cost. This has two important implications for the application of a fixed ratio rule to entities in large groups compared with other entities:

- Firstly, the analysis of financial data provided to the OECD during the public consultation on Action 4 indicates that large groups tend to have lower net third party interest/EBITDA ratios compared with other groups. For example, a benchmark fixed ratio of 30% would allow around 95% of publicly traded multinational groups with market capitalisation of USD 5 billion or above and with positive EBITDA to deduct all of their net third party interest expense, compared with around 85% of groups of all sizes. Therefore, to create a level playing field, a country may apply one benchmark fixed ratio to entities in large groups, and a higher benchmark fixed ratio to other entities.

- Secondly, because large groups are more likely to raise third party debt centrally, they are less likely to be exposed to differences in interest rates in the countries in which they operate. Therefore, in setting a benchmark fixed ratio to apply to entities in large groups, a country should not take into account whether its interest rate is higher or lower than those in other countries (i.e. factor 4 above should not be taken into account).

107. Where a country applies a different benchmark fixed ratio to entities in large groups compared with other entities, the definition of a large group should be based on the position of an entity's worldwide group and not only the local group including entities in the country. Although the data referred to above defined a large group based on market capitalisation, it is not recommended that this definition be used to set a benchmark fixed ratio. For privately held groups, a definition based on market capitalisation could not be applied. For publicly held groups, market capitalisation depends on many factors other than the group's level of economic activity. It is therefore suggested that a country's definition of a large group should be based on group consolidated revenue or group assets. Information on a group's consolidated revenue or assets may be obtained from the group's consolidated financial statements or directly from entities in the group where consolidated financial statements are not prepared. Information provided for the purposes of Country-by-Country reporting (*Transfer Pricing Documentation and Country-by-Country Reporting* (OECD, 2015)) may be used as a risk assessment tool to identify groups which may exceed this threshold, although this information should not be used by itself in order to apply a lower benchmark fixed ratio. Where a country applies different benchmark fixed ratios to entities in large groups and to other entities, it should include provisions to accommodate groups which cross the threshold, for example through a merger or divestiture. Such transitional provisions should be available for at most three years, to give groups an opportunity to adjust their capital structures.

Other factors that may be taken into account

108. When setting a benchmark fixed ratio within the corridor of 10% to 30%, countries may also take into account other relevant factors in addition to those set out above. For example:

- A country may apply a higher ratio within the corridor where data shows that there are high levels of net interest expense or debt due to economic or business policies and not due to base erosion and profit shifting.
- A country may apply a higher ratio within the corridor where it applies a macro-economic policy to encourage third party lending not related to base erosion and profit shifting, to increase investment (e.g. in infrastructure).
- A country may apply either a higher ratio or a lower ratio within the corridor where this is justified by local data on the external gearing of its domestic groups or the worldwide gearing of multinational groups operating in the country. This local data may for instance be based on tax rather than accounting figures.
- A country may apply a lower ratio within the corridor where it wishes to apply a stricter approach to tackling base erosion and profit shifting involving interest.

109. However, a country should not take into account any factor which is inconsistent with this report, which introduces competition issues or which fails to take into account the level of base erosion and profit shifting risk involving interest in that country. For example:

- A country should not apply a higher ratio where it has high levels of net interest expense or debt compared to those in other countries, which does not have a non-tax justification.
- A country should not apply a higher ratio due to a policy of attracting international investment into a country through lenient interest limitation rules.

Applying factors to set a benchmark fixed ratio within the best practice corridor

110. It is recommended that a country uses the factors in this chapter, along with other relevant factors, to set its benchmark fixed ratio within the recommended corridor. A country may develop its own approach as to how to apply the factors in setting a ratio, including applying a different weighting to each factor depending upon the extent to which it applies. In all cases, a country is able to choose to apply a lower benchmark fixed ratio within the corridor.

111. Illustrations of ways in which a country could use the factors to set its benchmark fixed ratio within the recommended corridor are included as Example 5 in Annex D. These are intended to illustrate possible ways in which a country could apply the factors in this chapter, but are not exhaustive and a different approach may be used.

Changes over time

112. Interest rates change over time and given interest rates are currently at a low level compared with long term averages, it may be necessary for a benchmark ratio to reflect changing interest rate environments. At the same time, however, countries need to consider that an entity's capacity to serve its interest payments is independent of the interest rate environment and that an increase in interest rates should typically result in reduced levels of debt. In this context, academic studies have found that corporate taxpayers issue more debt when interest rates are at a low level compared with historically higher rates (Barry et al., 2008).

113. Countries are therefore not expected to change the benchmark fixed ratio over time, but they may choose to change the ratio where there is a significant change in interest rates. For example, academic studies suggest that a country's credit rating, which influences the interest rates a country has to pay, has a significant impact on the credit rating for corporate bonds (Borensztein, Cowan and Valenzuela, 2007). This suggests that where a country's credit rating undergoes a significant change the benchmark fixed ratio may also be adjusted. However, to provide taxpayers with stable benchmark fixed ratios, countries should consider making changes only on an exceptional basis.

114. Additionally, where a country opts to make adjustments to the benchmark fixed ratio the country should ensure that the ratio moves down as well as up. For example, say a country operates an interest/EBITDA fixed ratio rule with a benchmark fixed ratio of 15%. As a result of an economic crisis domestic interest rates increase sharply, increasing the interest rates for local businesses. To reflect this increase the government raises the benchmark fixed ratio from 15% to 20%. At the same time, the government makes

provision that when the interest rates return to pre-crisis levels the benchmark fixed ratio will automatically drop down to 15%.

Notes

1. The term "related party" is defined in Chapter 9.
2. Chapter 11 includes a summary of different approaches that a country may use in applying a fixed ratio rule to a local group, depending upon the structure of its tax system.
3. On 18 December 2014, the OECD released a Public Discussion Draft on Action 4 (see Public Discussion Draft - BEPS Action 4: Interest deductions and other financial payments (www.oecd.org/ctp/aggressive/discussion-draft-action-4-interest-deductions.pdf). As part of their response, BIAC provided financial data based on an analysis performed by PricewaterhouseCoopers (PwC) of net interest/EBITDA ratios for public companies (see "Comments received on Public Discussion Draft – BEPS Action 4: Interest deductions and other financial payments – Part 1" page 179 www.oecd.org/ctp/aggressive/public-comments-action-4-interest-deductions-other-financial-payments-part1.pdf). Following the public consultation PwC provided updated figures, included in Annex B.
4. See Table B.3 in Annex B.

Bibliography

Barry, C.B. et al. (2008), "Corporate debt issuance and the historical level of interest rates", *Financial Management*, Vol. 37, Financial Management Association International, pp. 413-430.

Borensztein, E., K. Cowan and P. Valenzuela (2007), "Sovereign Ceilings "Lite"? The Impact of Sovereign Ratings on Corporate Ratings in Emerging Market Economies", IMF Working Paper, No. 07/75, International Monetary Fund, Washington, DC.

OECD (2015), *Transfer Pricing Documentation and Country-by-Country Reporting, Action 13 - 2015 Final Report*, OECD/G20 Base Erosion and Profit Shifting Project, OECD Publishing, Paris, http://dx.doi.org/10.1787/9789264241480-en.

Chapter 7

Group ratio rule

Aim of a group ratio rule

115. Under the recommended fixed ratio rule, an entity or local group can deduct net interest expense up to a fixed percentage of its EBITDA.[1] However, a fixed ratio rule does not take into account the fact that groups in different sectors may be leveraged differently and, even without a sector bias, some groups are simply more highly leveraged. Therefore, if a fixed ratio rule is introduced in isolation, groups which have a net third party interest/EBITDA ratio above the benchmark fixed ratio would be unable to deduct all of their net third party interest expense. To reduce the impact on more highly leveraged groups, it is recommended that countries consider combining a fixed ratio rule as described in Chapter 6, with a group ratio rule. This would allow an entity in a highly leveraged group to deduct net interest expense in excess of the amount permitted under the fixed ratio rule, based on a relevant financial ratio of the worldwide group. This means that the benchmark fixed ratio can be kept low, in particular for entities in large multinational groups, making sure the fixed ratio rule is effective in combating base erosion and profit shifting, while the group ratio rule compensates for the blunt operation of such a rule.

116. A group ratio rule may be introduced as a separate additional provision, or as an integral part of an overall rule including a fixed ratio rule. For example, where a country applies an approach based on an entity's net interest/EBITDA ratio, a single rule could provide that an entity can deduct up to the higher of the benchmark fixed ratio and the group's ratio. The decision to implement the fixed ratio rule and group ratio rule separately or as parts of a single rule may depend upon how a country intends the different elements to operate. For example, a single rule with two parts may be easier to apply if a country determines that both the fixed ratio and group ratio elements should use the same calculation of entity EBITDA based on tax numbers, and the same carry forward/carry back provisions

117. This chapter contains a description of a best practice rule which allows an entity which exceeds the benchmark fixed ratio to deduct net interest expense up to its group's net third party interest/EBITDA ratio, if this is higher. Where the net interest/EBITDA ratio of an entity exceeds that of its group, the entity can claim deductions up to its group's ratio. Only net interest expense which exceeds both the benchmark fixed ratio and the ratio of its group should be disallowed. While a rule based on a net third party interest/EBITDA ratio should be effective in tackling base erosion and profit shifting, it is recognised that some groups are subject to legal or practical constraints that limit their ability to align net interest expense and EBITDA in each entity. For these groups, some of the elements within the best practice approach, such as applying an uplift to net third

party interest expense (discussed in the section on *Calculation of net third party interest expense* below), and carry forward/carry back provisions (discussed in Chapter 8), may reduce the impact of these constraints. Simple illustrations of how a group ratio rule in this form would allow an entity which exceeds the benchmark fixed ratio to deduct more interest expense up to its group's net third party interest/EBITDA ratio are included in Example 6 in Annex D. It is recognised that to date no country applies a group ratio rule based on this approach. Therefore, this report sets out a framework for a group ratio rule using a net third party interest/EBITDA ratio, but further technical work on the design and operation of such a rule will be undertaken and completed in 2016.

Option to apply different group ratio rules, or no group ratio rule

118. A number of countries currently apply a fixed ratio rule in combination with a group ratio rule using an assets-based ratio, such as equity/total assets. For example, under the "equity escape" rule applied in Finland and Germany (described in Annex C), the fixed ratio rule based on net interest/EBITDA does not apply if an entity can show that its equity/total assets ratio is equal to or exceeds that of its group (within a small tolerance). This approach has a stricter outcome for many groups as, where an entity is more highly leveraged than its group, it remains subject to the fixed ratio rule whereas, under the net third party interest/EBITDA rule described in this chapter, only net interest that exceeds both the benchmark fixed ratio and the group's ratio is disallowed. However, for a loss-making entity, the equity escape rule could be more generous, as the entity may still deduct its net interest expense if it can demonstrate that the requirements of the rule are met. Where a country applies a group ratio rule which differs from the net third party interest/EBITDA rule in this report, the country's rule is included in the best practice so long as it only permits an entity to exceed the benchmark fixed ratio based on a relevant financial ratio of its group (such as equity/total assets).

119. There will be cases where countries decide to apply a fixed ratio rule in isolation, without a group ratio rule. This could be because a country wishes to reduce the tax bias between funding using debt or equity for all entities; or where, for constitutional or other reasons, a country wants to apply the same benchmark fixed ratio to all entities, without reference to the leverage position of the wider group. Where a country does not apply a group ratio rule, it should apply the fixed ratio rule consistently to entities in multinational and domestic groups, without improper discrimination.

120. Whether a country applies the group ratio rule described in this chapter, a different group ratio rule, or no group ratio rule, in all cases, a best practice approach must include a fixed ratio rule with a benchmark fixed ratio set within the corridor and based on the factors described in Chapter 6.

Obtaining financial information on a group

121. The group ratio rule requires an entity to be able to determine the net third party interest/EBITDA ratio of its worldwide group. This means that an entity must obtain information on its group which can be audited by its local tax authority, reducing the need for the local tax authority to obtain information from tax authorities in other countries. Therefore, it is important that a best practice approach be designed with this need in mind, so that a rule can be reasonably simple to apply by groups and tax authorities. Where an entity is unable to obtain information on its group necessary to apply the group

ratio rule, it can still apply the fixed ratio rule and deduct interest up to the benchmark fixed ratio.

122. Consolidated financial statements provide the most reliable source of financial information on a worldwide group. Therefore, where possible, the group information required to apply a group ratio rule should be taken from a group's consolidated financial statements. A national tax authority will typically not be in a position to confirm the accuracy of group financial data, and so it is recommended that consolidated financial statements should be audited by an independent regulated accountant. However, a country may allow unaudited financial statements to be used so long as these are subject to some form of reliable independent confirmation, or are reviewed by the tax authority.

123. It is recommended that, as a minimum, countries should accept consolidated financial statements prepared under local Generally Accepted Accounting Principles (GAAP) and the most common accounting standards used by large listed multinational groups (i.e. International Financial Reporting Standards (IFRS), Japanese GAAP and US GAAP). In order to enable non-listed groups to prepare a single set of consolidated financial statements for use in all countries in which they operate, countries should consider accepting consolidated financial statements prepared under other accounting standards, but it is left to each country to determine which accounting standards to accept (e.g. taking into account the geographical region and main sources of foreign investment).

124. For most listed groups and many unlisted groups, audited consolidated financial statements will be available from public sources including the group's website. In other cases, consolidated financial statements will need to be provided directly to the tax authority by entities in a group. In some cases, a tax authority may wish to use exchange of information provisions in applicable international agreements to confirm with the tax authority in the country of the group's parent company that the consolidated financial statements they have been provided with are the same as those provided by the parent, to ensure the group is using the same consolidated numbers in different countries.

Definition of a group

125. Given consolidated financial statements provide the most complete and objective source of financial information on multinational groups, a practical and workable definition of a group is one that is based on a consolidated group for financial accounting purposes. Therefore, for the purposes of applying a group ratio rule, a group includes a parent company and all entities which are fully consolidated on a line-by-line basis in the parent's consolidated financial statements.

126. In general, the parent should be the top level company in a holding structure. Where a group prepares consolidated financial statements at different levels (e.g. for local reporting or regulatory purposes), the group will be based on the consolidated financial statements prepared by the top level company (i.e. the highest level of consolidation). A group cannot be headed by an individual or entity other than a company. A group does not include entities which are included in the consolidated financial statements but are not fully consolidated on a line-by-line basis. In other words, it does not include entities which are included using equity accounting, proportionate consolidation or at fair value. In limited situations, an entity may be controlled by a company but not consolidated in that company's consolidated financial statements. This may arise for example where the company is an investment entity which makes investments for the purposes of capital appreciation and/or investment income, and may account for these investments at fair

value. In these situations, even though the controlled entity is not the top level company in the holding structure, it may be the parent of a separate group (including itself and any entities that it includes in its consolidated financial statements). Illustrations of how this definition would apply to groups in different scenarios are included as Example 7 in Annex D.

127. As set out in Chapter 9, a group ratio rule should be supported by a targeted rule to address the risk that a group ratio could be inflated using interest paid to a related party outside the group.[2] A targeted rule should be an effective solution to this risk, and also has the benefit that only groups which make interest payments to related parties would be required to make an adjustment under the rule. However, a country may choose to address this risk by including specified related parties, such as those under the common control of an individual or non-corporate entity, within the definition of a group. This approach is currently taken by some countries which apply a group ratio rule based on an equity/total assets ratio. A country may also address this risk by excluding all interest paid to related parties from the calculation of the group's net third party interest expense (as set out in the section *Calculation of net third party interest expense* below).

128. Where a country applies the best practice approach to the position of the local group rather than to each entity separately, attention will need to be paid to issues arising from differences between a group for financial reporting purposes (which in broad terms is based on a 50% control test) and a group for tax purposes (which is usually based on a higher level of control). A country's local group for the purposes of applying the group ratio rule may therefore include entities which are not included in a group for other tax purposes. Where this is the case, the interaction with, for example, tax consolidation, loss surrender and profit contribution rules may need to be considered. These issues are considered in Chapter 11.

Operation of a group ratio rule

129. Determining the amount of net interest expense deductible under a group ratio rule involves a two stage test.

1. Determine the group's net third party interest/EBITDA ratio

Net third party interest expense / Group EBITDA = Group ratio

2. Apply the group's ratio to an entity's EBITDA

Group ratio x Entity EBITDA = Limit on net interest deductions

Stage 1: Determine the group's net third party interest/EBITDA ratio

130. The first stage in applying the group ratio rule is to calculate the worldwide group's net third party interest/EBITDA ratio. To ensure that a rule is as straightforward as possible for a group to apply and for tax authorities to audit, this should be based on information which can be obtained from the group's consolidated financial statements.

Calculation of net third party interest expense

131. As described in Chapter 2, a best practice approach should address base erosion and profit shifting involving interest and payments economically equivalent to interest. Accounting standards vary in their treatment of a group's financial income and expenses, but most take a broad approach which includes interest and payments economically equivalent to interest. It is therefore recommended that when calculating a group's net third party interest/EBITDA ratio, net third party interest expense should be based on financial accounting figures.

132. Within this approach, a group's net third party interest expense could be determined in three ways. These represent increasing degrees of accuracy but, at the same time, increasing degrees of complexity.

Approach 1: Using unadjusted financial reporting figures

133. The most straightforward approach to determining net third party interest expense would be to take income and expense figures directly from a group's consolidated financial statements without adjustment. Depending upon the accounting standards and policies applied, these may be described as interest income and expense, finance income and expense, or a similar term. This would be a simple approach to apply which in many cases should provide effective protection against serious base erosion and profit shifting. However, a risk remains as using unadjusted figures could mean that a group's net third party interest expense may be overstated or understated, resulting in a limit on an entity's net interest deductions which is too high (giving rise to possible base erosion and profit shifting) or too low (giving rise to double taxation). This approach would also mean that a group's net third party interest expense would vary depending on the accounting standards applied, and the ability for interest income or expense to be included in a different line of the group's income statement. For example, in some cases accounting standards allow flexibility for certain items of income and expense to be recognised in operating profit, in finance income and expense, or as a separate item on the face of the consolidated income statement. Finally, using unadjusted figures could result in significant volatility in a group's net third party interest expense, for example where a group preparing consolidated financial statements under IFRS includes fair value movements on financial assets and liabilities within finance income and expense.

Approach 2: Using financial reporting figures adjusted for certain amounts

134. Rather than using figures taken directly from a group's consolidated financial statements without adjustment, a country could require an entity to make adjustments to include or exclude certain payments. This would result in a slightly more complex rule, but one which addresses some of the differences between accounting standards and more accurately reflects the amounts described in Chapter 2. Possible adjustments which a country could require an entity to make in determining net third party interest expense include the following:

- **The removal of payments which are not economically equivalent to interest.** This could include (i) dividend income, (ii) gains and losses on the disposal of financial instruments, (iii) fair value gains and losses on financial instruments, and (iv) notional interest amounts which do not include actual payments of interest. In many cases these amounts may be identified in a group's consolidated financial statements.

- **The addition of capitalised interest.** Capitalised interest is included in the balance sheet valuation of an asset and is not included in the group's finance expense. The amount of interest capitalised in a year will often be identified in a group's consolidated financial statements. An adjustment for capitalised interest may be made in the period where the interest is incurred, or as it is amortised over the life of the related asset.
- **The addition of interest income or expense recognised within a different category of income or expense.** This could include interest income which is included within gross revenue, or interest expense which is included within cost of sales or in the tax line. In some cases these amounts may not be identified in a group's consolidated financial statements, and will need to be obtained from underlying financial information. Groups may be able to introduce processes to identify these payments more easily, in particular where this would mean an increase in total net third party interest expense.

135. Where a country applies this approach, it could require an entity to have the amount of each adjustment to be confirmed by an independent regulated accountant. Alternatively a tax authority may conduct its own enquiries to confirm the adjustments.

Approach 3: Using a financial reporting valuation of interest and other payments specified in Chapter 2

136. The most accurate, but potentially the most complex, approach would be to require an entity to provide a valuation of the amounts included in the definition of interest and payments economically equivalent to interest set out in Chapter 2, based on the amounts included in its group's consolidated financial statements.

137. In most cases this should give substantially the same value for net third party interest expense as under Approach 2. However, where there is a difference between the items included in a group's finance income and expense and those included in the definition contained in Chapter 2, which is not represented by adjustments set out above, this approach should give the more precise and targeted result. On the other hand, it may be more difficult for this value of net third party interest expense to be confirmed directly using a group's consolidated financial statements and so this approach should only be used if a country is confident that it is able to audit a group's underlying books and records.

Proposed approach

138. The calculation of net third party interest income should be based on figures taken from a group's consolidated financial statements. While the use of unadjusted figures is currently considered an acceptable approach, there are risks that net third party interest expense could be overstated or understated and it is likely that most countries will wish to make some adjustments to these figures, although in the interests of simplicity these adjustments should be kept to a minimum. Further work is required to assess the feasibility of each of the above approaches, how information may be obtained from financial statements prepared under different accounting standards and, where adjustments to financial reporting figures are to be made, what amounts should be included and excluded from net third party interest expense.

139. Under all three approaches, a country can choose to allow an uplift of net third party interest expense of up to 10%. This would reduce the risk that all of a group's actual

net third party interest expense is not taken into account. It would also reduce the impact of constraints which mean that, even in the long term, a group may not be able to precisely align its net interest expense and EBITDA. An illustration of how an uplift could be applied is included in Example 6c in Annex D.

140. As discussed above in the section on *Definition of a group*, under a group ratio rule there is a risk that a group's net third party interest expense may be inflated using interest paid to related parties outside the group. This would have the effect of increasing the group's net third party interest/EBITDA ratio, and increase the limit on net interest deductions applicable to each group entity. A country may address this risk by providing that net third party interest expense should exclude any payments made to related parties. Alternatively, where a country allows interest paid to related parties to be included in net third party interest expense, it should introduce targeted rules as described in Chapter 9 to ensure that these payments are not used to reduce the effectiveness of the rule in tackling base erosion and profit shifting.

Calculation of group EBITDA

141. EBITDA is an objective measure of economic activity in a group, which can be applied to groups operating in most sectors (with the exception of the banking and insurance sectors, which are considered in Chapter 10). EBITDA is not generally included on the face of a group's consolidated income statement, but for the purposes of applying a group ratio rule, it should be calculated using figures which are readily available from a group's consolidated financial statements.

142. Within a best practice, as a starting point group EBITDA should be profit before tax plus net third party interest expense, depreciation and amortisation (including impairment charges). To avoid double counting, where net third party interest expense has been adjusted to include capitalised interest (or the amortisation of capitalised interest), depreciation and amortisation should be adjusted to strip out any amounts that represent the amortisation of interest included in the value of capitalised assets. Further work will be conducted to refine the definition of group EBITDA, including for example whether or not it should exclude items such as dividend income (and whether this should be dependent on if the dividends would be taxable if received in the country applying the rule), other finance income and expense not included in net third party interest expense, one-off items resulting from restructurings and mergers, and the share of profit from associates and joint venture entities which are included in the consolidated financial accounts under equity accounting but are not part of the group for group ratio rule purposes.[3]

Stage 2: Apply the group's ratio to an entity's EBITDA

143. Once a group's net third party interest expense and EBITDA have been established, it is possible to calculate the group's net third party interest/EBITDA ratio. This ratio may then be applied to the EBITDA of an individual entity within a group to determine the limit on net interest deductions that may be claimed under a group ratio rule. Within the best practice, a country may provide for entity EBITDA to be calculated using either tax or accounting principles. A summary of how to determine an entity's tax-EBITDA and accounting-EBITDA under a best practice approach is set out below. More detail, including illustrations of how these approaches may give rise to different results, is included in Example 8 in Annex D.

Determining an entity's tax-EBITDA

144. An entity's tax-EBITDA is equal to its taxable profit after adding back tax values for net interest expense, depreciation and amortisation. These values are determined under the tax rules of the country applying the rule. Non-taxable income such as branch profits or dividend income that benefit from a participation exemption should not be included within tax-EBITDA. Appropriate adjustments should also be made for taxable branch profits and dividend income to the extent that they are shielded from tax by foreign tax credits, to address the base erosion and profit shifting issues which are the subject of this report. A group's net third party interest/EBITDA ratio can be applied to an entity's tax-EBITDA to give a tax-based limit on net interest deductions. This limit is compared directly to the entity's net interest expense for tax purposes to determine the amount which may be deducted.

145. Determining EBITDA using tax principles is consistent with the approach recommended for calculating entity earnings under the fixed ratio rule. It is also straightforward for groups to apply and tax authorities to audit, and as an approach to tackle base erosion and profit shifting it has the benefit that an entity's interest deductions are linked to its level of taxable income. This means that where an entity's taxable income is higher than its accounting income, its ability to deduct interest expense will be correspondingly greater. Similarly, if an entity undertakes planning to reduce its taxable income, it will be able to deduct less net interest expense. Where a country applies the group ratio rule to the position of the local group, rather than to each entity separately, the local group's tax-EBITDA should be reasonably straightforward to calculate, by aggregating the tax-EBITDA of each entity (with adjustment where a local group includes entities which have different periods for tax purposes).

Determining an entity's accounting-EBITDA

146. An entity's accounting-EBITDA should be determined using the same formula as for group EBITDA. However, any income which is not subject to tax, such as dividends or branch profits which fall within a participation exemption, should be excluded. This is to ensure that an entity does not attract a higher level of interest capacity as a result of receiving tax exempt income, which could give rise to base erosion and profit shifting.

147. In principle, an entity's accounting-EBITDA should be based on financial reporting figures prepared under the same accounting rules as used in the consolidated financial statements. However, for many groups this would impose a significant burden, as entity financial statements may only currently be prepared under local GAAP. Therefore, in light of the fact that for groups in most sectors the elements of EBITDA are recognised and valued in a broadly consistent way under the main accounting standards, countries should consider accepting entity EBITDA prepared under local GAAP as a practical alternative. In deciding whether to accept entity EBITDA prepared under local GAAP, a country may consider the extent to which local GAAP is aligned with IFRS and other major accounting standards.

148. In determining an entity's accounting-EBITDA, it is also recommended that no adjustments should be made to strip out the profit or loss arising from intragroup transactions. This will mean that in some cases the aggregate EBITDA of the entities in a group may exceed the consolidated EBITDA of the group as a whole. This may arise, for example, where one entity in a group recognises the profit arising on the sale of goods to another group entity, but the purchase price is not included in the second entity's cost of sales as the goods have not yet been sold outside the group. However, this approach

should ensure that the EBITDA of each entity reflects its level of economic activity, even where this is a result of dealing within its group. Where a country applies the group ratio rule to the position of a local group as a whole, the accounting-EBITDA of the entities in the local group should be aggregated. In this case, to the extent intragroup transactions within the local group do not offset against each other, these may be eliminated.

149. A group's net third party interest/EBITDA ratio can be applied to an entity's accounting-EBITDA to give an accounts-based limit on net interest expense. This limit could be compared directly to the entity's net interest expense for tax purposes, to determine how much may be deducted. Alternatively, the accounts-based limit may be adjusted to take into account differences between the entity's net interest expense for accounting and tax purposes. A possible approach to achieve this is set out in Example 8c in Annex D.

Addressing the impact of loss-making entities on the operation of a group ratio rule

150. In general, under a group ratio rule an entity is able to claim deductions for interest expense up to the net third party interest/EBITDA ratio of its group. However there are two scenarios, both of which may arise as a result of the presence of loss-making entities within a group, which mean that this general approach needs to be limited.

151. The first scenario concerns a group which has a positive EBITDA, but this includes the results of a loss-making entity. The impact of this is that group EBITDA is reduced and the group's net third party interest/EBITDA ratio is increased. Under a group ratio rule, this would increase the capacity of profitable entities in the group to deduct interest expense, possibly to an extent that exceeds the actual net interest expense of the entire group. Where a carry forward of unused interest capacity is permitted, this interest capacity could be used to shelter interest deductions in future periods. This is illustrated by Example 9a in Annex D. This risk could be dealt with in part by a general principle that places an upper limit on the interest capacity of any entity applying the group ratio rule, equal to the net third party interest expense of the entire group. This upper limit should not mean that an entity's net interest deductions are lower than they would have been under the group ratio rule if group EBITDA had not been reduced by losses. This approach does not remove the risk that the total net interest deductions of all group entities could exceed the group's actual net third party interest expense. However, it should prevent an individual entity receiving a very high level of interest capacity that could be used for base erosion and profit shifting purposes. How this upper limit would operate is shown in Example 9b in Annex D.

152. The second scenario concerns groups which have negative EBITDA at a consolidated level, but which include some profitable entities. In this situation, it is not possible to calculate a meaningful net third party interest/EBITDA for the group, as the ratio will be negative. However, a profitable entity within the group is still making a positive contribution to the group's results, which should be recognised. In this case, under the best practice approach an entity with positive EBITDA which is part of a loss-making group could receive interest capacity equal to the lower of the entity's actual net interest expense and the net third party interest expense of the group. As shown in Example 9c in Annex D, this allows the entity to deduct its actual net interest expense, subject to an upper limit based on the actual net interest expense of its group. Given in these circumstances a group ratio cannot be calculated, this is the most straightforward way of linking an entity's interest deductibility to the position of its group.

153. An alternative approach would be to exclude loss-making entities from the calculation of a group's EBITDA. This would remove the risk that any entity would receive an excessive amount of interest capacity. However, in general it would not be possible to obtain information on loss-making entities within a group from the consolidated financial statements. It may be possible for an entity to provide this information directly to a country's tax authority, but it may be very difficult for the tax authority to confirm the accuracy of this information and ensure that all loss-making entities in a group have been identified and excluded. Illustrations of how this approach could operate in practice are shown in Examples 9d and 9e in Annex D.

154. Further work will be conducted on the impact of losses on the operation of a group ratio rule, and the feasibility of different approaches to address this impact. Issues surrounding the impact of losses on a group ratio rule only arise where the rule uses an earnings-based ratio. Where a different rule is applied such as one based on an equity/total assets ratio, there should be no need to have specific provisions to deal with the effect of losses.

Notes

1. Chapter 11 includes a summary of different approaches that a country may use in applying a fixed ratio rule to a local group, depending upon the structure of its tax system.

2. The term "related party" is defined in Chapter 9.

3. For financial reporting purposes, "associates" are entities over which a group has significant influence, but this influence is not sufficient for the group to exercise control. In broad terms, this is typically where a group controls between 20% and 50% of the voting power in the entity.

Chapter 8

Addressing volatility and double taxation

155. An important issue under a best practice approach which links net interest deductions to the level of an entity's EBITDA is how to deal with volatility in earnings which impacts an entity's ability to deduct its interest expense. Where earnings volatility or mismatches in the timing of interest expense and EBITDA result in an entity exceeding the benchmark fixed ratio under a fixed ratio rule, the group ratio rule described in Chapter 7 may provide a solution by allowing the entity to deduct net interest expense up to the group's net third party interest/EBITDA ratio where this is higher. This could also be achieved using a group ratio rule based on an equity/total assets ratio, such as an "equity escape rule" described in Annex C, which could also be used by an entity with negative EBITDA if it is able to demonstrate that the requirements of the rule are met. Otherwise, these issues may be addressed to an extent by using average EBITDA over a number of years or by permitting an entity to carry disallowed interest expense and unused interest capacity for use in earlier or later periods.

Measuring economic activity using average EBITDA

156. Rather than linking an entity's ability to deduct net interest expense to economic activity in a single year, the impact of short term volatility could be reduced through the use of average figures. For example, under a fixed ratio rule the ratio could be applied to the average of EBITDA in the current year and, say, the previous two years. In this case, the impact of a single year fall in EBITDA would be spread over a three year period, with the lower earnings in one year offset against higher earnings in other years. The use of averaging within a group ratio rule would be more complicated, as it would need to be used in calculating the EBITDA of the group as well as of each entity. This would give rise to additional issues that would need to be considered, such as how to deal with cases where the composition of a group changes during the period used for calculating the average. However, the use of averaging could reduce the impact of losses on the operation of a rule, in particular where an entity is only in a loss-making position for one or two years.

157. The use of averaging could provide an entity with some protection against short term volatility, but would provide no protection against longer term volatility outside of the period used for calculating an average. Averaging would also not help an entity which incurs interest expense to fund a project or investment that gives rise to EBITDA more than, say, two years later.

158. Overall, the use of averages is likely to make a rule more complex but it could help address volatility. Therefore, this is an option that countries may choose to apply under the best practice approach. However, to reduce the risk of arbitrage it is suggested that an election to use average figures should apply to all entities in a local group. An

illustration of how three year averaging could be applied to a fixed ratio rule is included as Example 10 in Annex D.

Carry forward and carry back of disallowed interest and unused interest capacity

159. Where a payment of interest relates to a specific transaction intended to give rise to base erosion or profit shifting, or the entity consistently has a level of net interest expense in excess of the benchmark fixed ratio and group ratio, a permanent disallowance of net interest expense may be an appropriate result. However, there may be cases where the amount of interest expense in an entity exceeds that which is allowable merely as a result of a timing mismatch which will correct in a future period. This may arise, for example, where an entity incurs interest expense to fund a project or investment that will give rise to earnings in a future period. There may also be cases where an entity's EBITDA fluctuates for reasons outside of its control, for example as a result of changing market conditions, increasing or reducing the amount of net interest expense it may deduct for tax. In addition, under a group ratio rule, the amount of net interest expense that an entity can deduct may be impacted by volatility in EBITDA elsewhere in the group. In these cases, a permanent disallowance of interest expense would introduce a level of uncertainty for groups which could make long term planning difficult and which a country may view as undesirable. A permanent disallowance of interest expense may also result in double taxation, if the lender is taxed on the corresponding interest income.

160. Both a fixed ratio rule and a group ratio rule establish a limit on the ability of an entity to deduct net interest expense (i.e. its interest capacity). Except in cases where an entity's interest capacity precisely matches its net interest expense, the operation of a rule will result in an entity either incurring an interest disallowance (i.e. where its net interest expense exceeds the maximum permitted), or having unused interest capacity (i.e. where its net interest expense is below the maximum permitted). Allowing disallowed interest expense and unused interest capacity to be used in other periods through carry forward or carry back provisions would have clear benefits for entities, reducing the risk of a permanent disallowance of interest expense where interest expense and EBITDA arise in different periods. From a country's perspective, this could also support a policy that the level of an entity's net interest deductions should be linked to its level of earnings over time.

161. Under the best practice approach, there is no requirement for a country to allow an entity to carry forward or carry back disallowed interest expense or unused interest capacity. However, a country may choose to allow an entity:

- to carry forward disallowed interest expense only
- to carry forward disallowed interest expense and unused interest capacity
- to carry forward and carry back disallowed interest expense.

162. An entity's disallowed interest expense that may be carried forward or carried back under these provisions will generally be the deductible net interest expense that is in excess of the amount permitted under the fixed ratio rule and group ratio rule. Interest expense disallowed under targeted rules will generally relate to transactions or arrangements which give rise to specific base erosion and profit shifting risks, and should not be available for carry forward or carry back.

163. Where a country allows an entity to carry forward unused interest capacity, this may be limited to the amount by which an entity's net interest expense is below that permitted under the fixed ratio rule only. Alternatively, a country may allow the carry forward of unused interest capacity based on the level of net interest permitted under the group ratio rule. This would reduce the impact of volatility in group earnings on an entity's ability to deduct net interest expense, and is consistent with the principle of allowing a group to deduct an amount equivalent to its net third party interest expense. In either case, a carry forward of unused interest capacity could allow an entity that has already deducted all of its net interest expense to build up a potentially significant carry forward.

164. Allowing disallowed interest expense and unused interest capacity to be carried forward or back and used in other periods does introduce potential base erosion and profit shifting risks. This is particularly the case for unused interest capacity, where a long or unlimited carry forward could give rise to a sizeable tax asset which can only be realised either by increasing the level of the entity's net interest expense, or by reducing the level of EBITDA in a future period, neither of which should be incentivised by a rule to tackle base erosion and profit shifting. Similar concerns exist with respect to carry backs of disallowed interest expense. On the other hand, a long or unlimited carry forward of disallowed interest expense could encourage an entity to increase its interest expense up to the maximum amount permitted, in the knowledge that if it exceeds the amount of interest allowed in a year, the surplus may be deducted in future periods. However, this risk is not judged to be as significant as the risks associated with a carry back of disallowed interest expense or carry forward of unused interest capacity, as these latter types of carry over provisions offer greater possibility of immediate monetisation.

165. Therefore, where carry forwards or carry backs are permitted, a country may consider imposing limits in terms of time and/or value. This is particularly important with respect to a carry forward of unused interest capacity and carry back of disallowed interest expense, which give rise to greater potential base erosion and profit shifting risks. Limits on carry forwards and carry backs could include the following:

- The number of years for which disallowed interest expense or unused interest capacity may be carried forward, or disallowed interest expense may be carried back, could be limited.
- The value of carry forwards could reduce over time (e.g. by 10% each year).
- The value of a carry forward or carry back could be capped at a fixed monetary amount.
- The amount of a carry forward or carry back that may be used in a single year could be limited (e.g. providing that no more than 50% of current net interest expense may be set against unused interest capacity carried forward from previous years).
- Carry forwards should be reset to zero in certain circumstances, following normal practice applied to loss carry forwards (e.g. where a company changes ownership and also changes the nature of its economic activity).

166. Where a country applies a fixed ratio rule in combination with a group ratio rule, it may apply a single carry forward provision to deal with disallowed interest under both rules. Alternatively, a country could impose different limits depending upon whether interest expense is disallowed under the fixed ratio rule or the group ratio rule. However,

this approach is likely to be considerably more complex to apply and administer. For example, groups may be required to maintain a separate carry forward pool under each rule. The country would also need to consider how disallowed interest carried forward in each pool can be used (e.g. whether one pool should be used first, or whether interest disallowed under one rule may only be set against interest capacity arising under the same rule).

167. Where a country applies interest limitation rules to the position of the local group rather than each entity separately, it should also consider how this will impact any carry forward or carry back provisions (e.g. whether an entity should be able to utilise disallowed interest expense carried forward from a period prior to the time it joined the group).

Chapter 9

Targeted rules

Aim of targeted rules

168. Targeted interest limitation rules include any provisions which apply to restrict interest deductions on payments made under specific transactions or arrangements. These may be contrasted with general interest limitation rules, such as the fixed ratio rule and group ratio rule, which impose an overall limit on an entity's interest deductions. A number of countries do not currently apply any general interest limitation rule and rely solely on targeted rules. One benefit of such an approach is that it reduces the risk that a rule could negatively impact on entities which are already appropriately capitalised and also avoids any incentive for groups to increase the level of net interest expense of local entities up to the level allowed under a fixed ratio rule. The use of targeted rules also allows countries to address specific areas of concern, potentially minimising compliance costs for entities, in particular those which do not engage in base erosion or profit shifting. However, such an approach has drawbacks. Most importantly, to some extent targeted rules will always be a reactive response, requiring countries to be aware of specific base erosion and profit shifting risks as they emerge. There is a risk that some groups may consider all arrangements not covered by targeted rules to be acceptable, meaning that over time new targeted rules may be required. Targeted rules also require active application, meaning the tax administration must be able to recognise situations where a rule could apply, often as part of a complex transaction, and then engage with a group to determine the correct result. Overall, an approach based entirely on targeted rules may result in a large number of rules which will increase complexity, as well as increasing compliance and administrative costs. If the rules are not comprehensive then they are unlikely to deal with all base erosion and profit shifting risks. On the other hand, an approach which uses a general rule supplemented by targeted rules in key areas should provide countries with the comfort that the main risks posed by base erosion and profit shifting are addressed, while ensuring that groups are able to obtain relief for their real net third party interest expense.

169. While the best practice approach in this report recommends general interest limitation rules, it is recognised that targeted rules can also provide an effective solution to some base erosion and profit shifting risk. This chapter sets out a number of specific risks that may not be addressed by the fixed ratio rule and group ratio rule, where targeted rules may be required. Countries may also continue to apply existing targeted and general interest limitation rules, where these address specific risks. For example, a country may apply a thin capitalisation rule based on a fixed debt/equity ratio to disallow interest on excessive debt in addition to the fixed ratio rule and this could apply to disallow interest even where an entity does not exceed the level of net interest expense permitted under the fixed ratio rule.

170. The impact of a targeted rule applying to an arrangement will vary depending upon the nature of the arrangement and the risk the rule is intended to address. In some cases it may be appropriate for a rule to deny a deduction for a gross interest payment under a transaction. In other cases it may be more appropriate for a rule to apply to part of a payment, or to net interest payments after taking into account income under the same transaction. Where the result of a transaction is to increase the level of net third party interest expense under a group ratio rule, a rule may simply operate to disregard this increase, with no specific disallowance.

Targeted rules to prevent avoidance of the general rules

171. A best practice approach should be robust against attempts to avoid the effect of a rule. A fixed ratio rule (and group ratio rule where applied) should therefore be supported by targeted rules to counteract planning undertaken by groups to reduce the impact of these rules. To achieve this, it is recommended that countries also introduce targeted rules to address the following risks:

- An entity with net interest expense enters into an arrangement to reduce the net interest expense subject to the fixed ratio rule (e.g. by converting interest expense into a different form of deductible expense, or by converting other taxable income into a form which is economically equivalent to interest).
- An entity which is part of a group enters into an arrangement with a related party or third party in order to increase the level of net third party interest expense under the group ratio rule (e.g. by making a payment to a related party or to a third party under a structured arrangement, or by converting interest income into a different form).
- A group is restructured to place an unincorporated holding entity at the top of the structure, to create two groups. This may be to prevent a fixed ratio rule applying (e.g. in a country where the rule does not apply to standalone entities) or to separate the original group into two parts for group ratio rule purposes.

172. The above risks may be addressed by standalone rules, specific provisions within the fixed ratio rule and group ratio rule, or by other tax rules (such as, for example, a country's general anti-avoidance rule). These rules should be applicable to all entities which are subject to the fixed ratio rule, and group ratio rule where this applies. The terms "related party" and "structured arrangement" are defined below.

Targeted rules to address other base erosion and profit shifting risks

173. The fixed ratio rule and group ratio rule described in this report provide an effective solution to tackle most base erosion and profit shifting involving interest and payments economically equivalent to interest. However, as set out in Chapter 3, in certain situations, a country may restrict application of the fixed ratio rule and group ratio rule to entities in multinational groups. Therefore, targeted rules may be required to address base erosion and profit shifting risks posed by entities which are not subject to the general interest limitation rules. Even where the fixed ratio rule and group ratio rule apply, a number of specific base erosion and profit shifting risks remain. Therefore, it is recommended that countries consider introducing rules to address the risks listed below:

- An entity which would otherwise have net interest income enters into an arrangement which involves the payment of interest to a group entity outside the country or a related party to reduce the level of interest income subject to tax in the country.

- An entity makes a payment of interest on an "artificial loan", where no new funding is raised by the entity or its group.
- An entity makes a payment of interest to a third party under a structured arrangement, for instance under a back-to-back arrangement.
- An entity makes a payment of interest to a related party, which is excessive or is used to finance the production of tax exempt income.
- An entity makes a payment of interest to a related party, which is subject to no or low taxation on the corresponding interest income.

174. Rules to address the risks above should ideally be applicable to all entities, irrespective of whether they are also subject to the fixed ratio rule and group ratio rule. However, these rules are particularly important where an entity is not subject to a fixed ratio rule as described in Chapter 6.

Definition of "related parties" and "structured arrangements"

175. A number of the specific risks listed above refer to transactions with or payments made to a related party or to a third party under a structured arrangement.

Related parties

176. An entity which is part of a group may also be related to individuals or entities which are not part of the group, but where a significant relationship exists. For the purposes of this report, two persons (including individuals and entities) are related if they are not in the same group but they meet any of the following conditions:

- The first person has an investment that provides that person with effective control of the second person or there is a third person that holds investments which provide that person with effective control over both persons.
- The first person has a 25% or greater investment in the second person or there is a third person that holds a 25% or greater investment in both.
- They can be regarded as associated enterprises under Article 9.

177. A person will be treated as holding a percentage investment in another person if that person holds directly or indirectly through an investment in other persons, a percentage of the voting rights of that person or of the value of any equity interests of that person.

178. For the purposes of this related party definition, a person who acts together with another person in respect of the ownership or control of any voting rights or equity interests will be treated as owning or controlling all of those voting rights and equity instruments.

179. Two persons will be treated as acting together in respect of ownership or control of any voting rights or equity interests if they meet any of the following conditions:

- They are members of the same family.

- One person regularly acts in accordance with the wishes of the other person in respect of ownership or control of such rights or interests.
- They have entered into an arrangement that has material impact on the value or control of any such rights or interests.
- They each directly or indirectly hold debt in the entity in proportion to their voting rights or equity interests.
- The ownership or control of any such rights or interests is managed by the same person or group of persons. In respect of any taxpayer that is a collective investment vehicle (CIV), if the investment manager can establish to the satisfaction of the tax authority from the terms of the investment mandate and the circumstances in which the investment was made that two funds were not acting together in respect of the investment, then the interests held by those funds should not be aggregated under this part of the "acting together" test.

180. For these purposes a CIV is any vehicle which is widely held, holds a diversified portfolio of securities and is subject to investor-protection regulation in the country in which it is established. It is left to countries to determine the types of vehicle which would meet this definition. For example, countries may consider certain types of CIVs to be widely-held if their shares or units are listed for quotation on a stock exchange or can be readily purchased or sold by the public (i.e. the purchase or sale of shares or units is not implicitly or explicitly restricted to a limited group of investors). However, a country may apply a different test to determine whether a CIV is widely held.

Structured arrangements

181. Targeted rules may also apply where an entity makes a payment of interest to a third party under a structured arrangement. A structured arrangement is any arrangement where the entity, its group and its related parties, taken together, do not bear the entire cost of the interest payment.

182. An example of a structured arrangement would be a "back-to-back" arrangement whereby an entity makes a payment of interest to a third party in circumstances where the third party also makes a payment to the entity, a member of the entity's group or a related party of the entity. This second payment may be in a form other than interest.

Chapter 10

Applying the best practice approach to banking and insurance groups

183. In developing a best practice approach to combat base erosion and profit shifting involving interest, a number of particular features of groups in the banking and insurance sectors need to be taken into account.

184. An important consideration is that the role interest plays in a banking or insurance business is different to that in other sectors. Banks and insurance companies hold financial assets and liabilities as an integral part of their main business activities. In addition, financial sector businesses in most countries are subject to strict regulations which impose restrictions on their capital structure. In 2011, Basel III introduced a leverage ratio standard intended to constrain leverage in the banking sector, helping to mitigate risks which in the past have damaged the financial system and the economy.[1] The Solvency II Directive introduces a similar system for insurers in the European Union.[2] It should be noted however that, although banking and insurance groups are subject to regulation, not all entities within a group are subject to the same obligations and the treatment of branches in particular must be taken into account.

185. Despite the restrictions imposed by regulatory requirements, a number of studies have found that the leverage of banks is influenced on average by corporate taxes to the same extent as for groups in other sectors. The influence of tax on leverage is reduced where a bank is capital constrained, but in practice many groups hold a buffer of capital above the minimum amount required by regulations (Heckemeyer and de Mooij, 2013; Keen and de Mooij, 2012).

186. Base erosion and profit shifting by banking and insurance groups could potentially take a number of forms. These include: regulated entities holding a regulatory capital buffer (including a debt component) above the level required to support existing business; routing regulatory capital and ordinary debt issued within a group through intermediate entities in low tax countries, placing excessive interest deductions in branches, which do not need to be separately capitalised for regulatory purposes, and in non-regulated entities; using deductible interest expense to fund assets which are tax exempt or taxed on a preferential basis; and the use of hybrid financial instruments and hybrid entities.

187. Banks and insurance companies typically hold buffers of regulatory capital above the minimum level required, and there are significant commercial drivers to maintain these buffers (e.g. connected to credit rating and cost of capital). Holding capital above the minimum required by regulations allows a group to accommodate changing capital needs, but also provides some opportunities for base erosion and profit shifting.

188. The fixed ratio rule and group ratio rule set out in this report are unlikely to be effective in addressing these base erosion and profit shifting risks for a number of reasons. In particular, banking and insurance groups are important sources of debt

funding for groups in other sectors and as such many are net lenders by a significant margin. This means that the main operating companies in these groups, and the groups overall, will often have net interest income rather than net interest expense. As the fixed ratio rule and group ratio rule apply to limit the level of an entity's net interest expense, these rules would have no impact on important entities within banking and insurance groups. In addition, the fact that interest income is a major part of a bank or insurance company's income means that EBITDA would not be a suitable measure for economic activity across a group in these sectors. Finally, the financial statements of banking and insurance groups typically differ from those of groups in other sectors, which in particular could impact the operation of a group ratio rule. As a fixed ratio rule and group ratio rule in this report are unlikely to address base erosion and profit shifting in the banking and insurance sectors, countries may consider excluding entities in groups operating in these sectors from the scope of these rules, in which case they should introduce targeted rules addressing base erosion and profit shifting in these sectors (as discussed below).

189. Any exclusion should not apply to treasury companies, captive insurance companies or other non-regulated entities which carry out quasi-banking or other financial activities where there are no regulatory restraints, or to investment vehicles whether or not regulated. These entities should remain subject to the rules contained in the best practice approach.

190. It is not intended that entities operating in the banking and insurance sectors, or regulated banking or insurance entities within non-financial groups, should be exempted from the best practice approach to tackle base erosion and profit shifting involving interest. Instead, in order to tackle base erosion and profit shifting by groups in all sectors, it is essential that a best practice approach includes rules which are capable of addressing risks posed by different entities. Further work will therefore be conducted to be completed in 2016, to identify best practice rules to deal with the potential base erosion and profit shifting risks posed by banks and insurance companies, taking into account the particular features of these sectors. This will include work on regulated banking and insurance activities within non-financial groups (such as groups operating in the manufacturing or retail sector). In particular, it is crucial that any recommended interest limitation rules do not conflict with or reduce the effectiveness of capital regulation intended to reduce the risk of a future financial crisis. Where a country applies the fixed ratio rule set out in this report to entities in banking and insurance groups, the country should still apply the specific best practice rules to be designed to address the base erosion and profit shifting risks posed by these sectors.

Notes

1. The Third Basel Accord is a comprehensive set of reform measures, agreed upon by members of the Basel Committee on Banking Supervision, to strengthen the regulation, supervision and risk management of the banking sector (www.bis.org/bcbs/index.htm?m=3%7C14, accessed on 3 September 2015).

2. Directive 2009/138/EC of the European Parliament and of the Council of 25 November 2009 on the taking-up and pursuit of the business of Insurance and Reinsurance (Solvency II) [2009] OJ L335/1.

Bibliography

Heckemeyer, J. and R. de Mooij (2013), "Taxes and Corporate Debt: Are Banks any Different?", *IMF Working Paper*, No. 13/221, International Monetary Fund, Washington, DC.

Keen, M. and R. de Mooij (2012), "Debt, Taxes and Banks", *IMF Working Paper*, No. 12/48, International Monetary Fund, Washington, DC.

Chapter 11

Implementing the best practice approach

Implementation and co-ordination

191. This report includes recommendations for a best practice approach to tackle base erosion and profit shifting involving interest. As set out in Chapter 1, a country may supplement this approach with other general or targeted interest limitation rules, either to address base erosion and profit shifting risks it faces or to achieve wider tax policy aims.

192. Further work will be conducted on particular areas of the best practice approach for instance guidance on the detailed operation of the group ratio rule. Work will also be conducted on the design of special rules to address base erosion and profit shifting in the banking and insurance sectors, taking into account the specific issues that groups operating in these sectors face. This work will be completed in 2016.

193. The design and content of the best practice approach set out in this report, including the corridor for setting a benchmark fixed ratio and the optional exclusion for interest funding certain public-benefit projects, will initially be reviewed by countries involved in the BEPS Project by no later than the end of 2020. This review will include consideration of the experience of countries which have introduced rules in accordance with the best practice and the impact on the behaviour of groups. The review will also consider any additional available data that could assist in assessing the effectiveness of the agreed corridor. To this end, countries are encouraged to collect tax data on the level of net interest expense and EBITDA of entities and local groups in that country, as well as those of multinational groups operating in the country where available. Following this review, elements of the best practice may be revised.

Transitional rules

194. The best practice approach set out in the report should address base erosion and profit shifting involving interest. However, it is recognised that any rule to limit tax deductions for an entity's interest expense could involve a significant cost for some entities. Therefore, it is expected that a country introducing a fixed ratio rule and group ratio rule would give entities reasonable time to restructure existing financing arrangements before the rules come into effect.

195. A country may also apply transitional rules which exclude interest on certain existing loans from the scope of the rules, either for a fixed period or indefinitely. In this case it is recommended that these transitional rules are primarily restricted to interest on third party loans entered into before the rules were announced. Interest on any loans entered into after the announcement of the new rules should not benefit from any transitional provisions. Alternatively, a country may apply no transitional rules.

Separate entity and group taxation systems

196. Countries currently apply corporate tax systems which include different types of group taxation and separate entity taxation. The best practice approach described in this report should be compatible with any system, although in some cases specific provisions within the best practice approach may require adjustment.

Countries applying separate entity taxation systems

197. Where a country taxes each entity within a group separately, the fixed ratio rule and group ratio rule may be applied in any of the following three ways at the discretion of the country:

- The fixed ratio rule and group ratio rule may be applied separately to each entity based on its EBITDA.
- The country may treat entities within a tax group as a single entity for the purposes of applying the fixed ratio rule and group ratio rule. For example, the benchmark fixed ratio would be applied to the tax group's total tax-EBITDA. Interest capacity would then be allocated within the tax group in accordance with rules developed by the country, which may include allowing a group to determine the allocation of interest capacity between entities. To prevent abuse, transactions within the tax group which do not net off may be stripped out of the tax group's "entity EBITDA". Under this option, entities which are in the same financial reporting group, but which are not part of the same tax group, would continue to be treated as separate entities and would apply the fixed ratio rule and group ratio rule independently.
- The country may treat all entities in the country which are part of the same financial reporting group as a single entity for the purposes of applying the fixed ratio rule and group ratio rule. Transactions within the financial reporting group which do not net off may be excluded from "entity EBITDA" to prevent abuse. This option may be particularly relevant for a country with a group ratio rule, which applies to entities in a financial reporting group. However, as this could in effect allow the transfer of interest capacity between entities which are not in a tax group, the country may need to consider whether this raises any policy concerns (such as inconsistency with existing loss surrender, profit contribution or similar rules). The operation of other provisions such as carry forwards and carry backs would need to be considered, for example whether an entity should be able to benefit from attributes carried forward from a period before it joined the financial reporting group.

Countries applying group taxation systems

198. Where a country taxes entities on a group or consolidated basis, the fixed ratio rule and group ratio rule may be applied in any of the following ways at the discretion of the country:

- The country may treat entities within the consolidated tax group as a single entity for the purposes of applying the fixed ratio rule and group ratio rule. For example, the benchmark fixed ratio would be applied to the consolidated tax group's total tax-EBITDA, and the amount of interest capacity applied to calculate the permitted net interest deductions for the consolidated tax group as a whole. Under this option, entities which are in the same financial reporting group, but which are not part of the same consolidated tax group, would continue to be treated as separate entities and would apply the fixed ratio rule and group ratio rule independently.

- The country may treat all entities in the country which are part of the same financial reporting group as a single entity for the purposes of applying the fixed ratio rule and group ratio rule. Transactions within the financial reporting group which do not net off may be excluded from "entity EBITDA" to prevent abuse. This option may be particularly relevant for a country with a group ratio rule, which applies to entities in a financial reporting group. However, as this could in effect allow the transfer of interest capacity between a consolidated tax group and an entity outside of that group, the country may need to consider whether this raises any policy concerns. The operation of other provisions such as carry forwards and carry backs would need to be considered, for example whether an entity should be able to benefit from attributes carried forward from a period before it joined the financial reporting group.

Interaction of the best practice approach with hybrid mismatch rules under Action 2

199. Where a country has introduced a fixed ratio rule, the potential base erosion and profit shifting risk posed by hybrid mismatch arrangements is reduced, as the overall level of net interest deductions an entity may claim is restricted. However, this risk is not eliminated. Within the limits imposed by a fixed ratio rule, there may still be significant scope for an entity to claim interest deductions in circumstances where a hybrid financial instrument or hybrid entity is used to give rise to a double deduction or deduction/no inclusion outcome. Where a group ratio rule applies, there is also a risk that hybrid mismatch arrangements could be used to increase a group's net third party interest expense, supporting a higher level of net interest deductions across the group. In order to address these risks, a country should implement all of the recommendations under Action 2, alongside the best practice approach in this report.

200. Rules to address hybrid mismatch arrangements should be applied by an entity before the fixed ratio rule and group ratio rule to determine an entity's total net interest expense. Once this total net interest expense figure has been determined, the fixed ratio rule and group ratio rule should be applied to establish whether the full amount may be deducted, or to what extent net interest expense should be disallowed.

201. The OECD Report, *Neutralising the Effects of Hybrid Mismatch Arrangements* (OECD, 2014) stated that rules which grant deemed interest deductions for equity capital, or have similar effect, would not be considered under Action 2, but should be considered further either separately or in the context of Action 4. As set out in Chapter 2, deemed deductions which are calculated by applying a specified percentage to the equity capital of an entity are not treated as being interest or a payment economically equivalent to interest for the purposes of this report. However, these rules should be considered further by the OECD in separate work.

Interaction of the best practice approach with controlled foreign company rules under Action 3

202. The fixed ratio rule and group ratio rule should be effective in addressing base erosion and profit shifting involving excessive interest deductions and interest used to

finance the production of tax exempt income. A country may also introduce controlled foreign company (CFC) rules in accordance with the recommendations under Action 3 (*Designing Effective Controlled Foreign Companies Rules* (OECD, 2015)), to address situations where an entity makes an interest payment which is deductible under the fixed ratio rule and group ratio rule, but the payment is made to a CFC which is subject to a low rate of tax.

203. Where a country applies CFC rules alongside interest limitation rules, CFC income which is subject to tax on the parent company may be included in the calculation of the parent's EBITDA when applying the fixed ratio rule and group ratio rule. Where this CFC income includes interest income or expense, the country should consider including the interest in the calculation of the parent's net interest expense and excluding that interest from the calculation of the parent's EBITDA.

204. The best practice approach in this report should also reduce the pressure on a country's CFC rules, by encouraging groups to spread net interest expense between group entities so that there is a greater link to taxable economic activity. This should reduce the level of net interest income arising in CFCs, as groups are likely to reduce the level of intragroup interest payments, and increase the alignment of net interest expense and EBITDA within the group.

Interaction of the best practice approach with other rules to limit interest deductions

205. As described in this report, a country may apply the fixed ratio rule and group ratio rule together with targeted rules to tackle specific base erosion and profit shifting risks, including the risks discussed in Chapter 9 as well as other risks identified by the country. A country may also apply other general interest limitation rules, such as arm's length rules, rules to disallow a percentage of all interest expense and thin capitalisation rules.

206. It is suggested that in most cases, these targeted and general interest limitation rules should be applied before the fixed ratio rule and group ratio rule. However, the ultimate decision as to the order in which to apply interest limitation rules is left to countries, taking into account the design of its rules and the risks they are intended to address.

Interaction of the best practice approach with withholding taxes

207. Withholding tax on interest is typically imposed in order to allocate taxing rights over income to a source country, although it is recognised that an effect of withholding taxes may be to reduce the benefits to groups of base erosion and profit shifting involving interest. Where a country applies withholding tax to payments of interest, this should in no way be impacted by the application of the fixed ratio rule, group ratio rule or targeted rules described in this report. Where the best practice approach limits an entity's net interest deductions, leading to an interest disallowance, there is no intention that the interest expense disallowed should be re-characterised for any other purpose. Therefore, to the extent a payment would be subject to withholding tax under a country's tax law, this would continue to apply. Where a country currently re-characterises disallowed interest, for example as a dividend payment, it may continue to apply this treatment but this is not part of the best practice approach in this report.

208. Where an entity receives interest net of withholding tax, and the country of the recipient allows a credit for this tax, the entity will typically be subject to tax on a gross amount of interest income including an amount representing the tax withheld. This treatment is not changed as a result of any aspect of the best practice approach. Therefore, where an entity would currently be able to claim credit for withholding tax on its interest income, this should not change following the introduction of the fixed ratio rule and group ratio rule.

Bibliography

OECD (2015), *Designing Effective Controlled Foreign Company Rules, Action 3 - 2015 Final Report*, OECD/G20 Base Erosion and Profit Shifting Project, OECD Publishing, Paris, http://dx.doi.org/10.1787/9789264241152-en.

OECD (2014), *Neutralising the Effects of Hybrid Mismatch Arrangements*, OECD Publishing, Paris, paragraph 4, http://dx.doi.org/10.1787/9789264218819-en.

Annex A

European Union Law issues

209. This annex includes a brief outline of EU law issues that EU Member States should take into account in implementing the best practice approach in this report.

EU treaty freedoms

210. The treaty freedoms that need to be considered in the context of interest limitation rules are the freedom of establishment, and the free movement of capital. The freedom of establishment applies to cases where the shareholder would be able to exercise a significant influence over the entity,[1] while the free movement of capital applies to cases where the shareholder acquired the shares for the sole purpose of making a financial investment without participating in the decision making process of the entity. In addition, the freedom to provide services, which also has to be analysed from the perspective of both the service provider and recipient, may also need to be considered.

211. The scope of an interest limitation rule determines which freedom applies and there are a number of approaches that the countries involved in this work have discussed in order to avoid any restriction of EU treaty freedoms. In this respect, consideration should also be given to the circumstances in which EU Member States could justify a restriction of EU treaty freedoms, for example:

- the need to preserve the balanced allocation between EU Member States of the power to impose taxes
- the need to prevent tax avoidance and to combat artificial arrangements.

EU directives

212. There are two EU directives with relevance to interest deduction limitation rules within the European Union: the Parent Subsidiary Directive[2] and the Interest and Royalty Directive.[3] The Parent Subsidiary Directive eliminates cross-border withholding taxes on dividend payments made by a subsidiary to a parent company and also eliminates double taxation of such income at the level of the parent company. The directive may be relevant in cases where excessive interest is re-qualified as a dividend. In such cases, the re-qualified interest should be granted the benefits of the Parent Subsidiary Directive.

213. The Interest and Royalty Directive provides that interest and royalty payments arising in an EU Member State shall be exempt from any taxes imposed on those payments in that State, whether by deduction at source or by assessment. Disallowing a deduction for excessive interest could be considered as taxation of interest and, thus, fall within the scope of the directive. However, the Court of Justice of the European Union clarified that the directive only concerns the tax position of the interest creditor.[4] It seems

to follow that the deductibility of interest expenses at the level of the debtor entity may therefore be restricted.

EU State aid

214. EU State aid issues may arise if interest deductibility rules include specific exceptions for particular entities or sectors. The relevant treaty provision considers "any aid granted by a Member State or through State resources in any form whatsoever which distorts or threatens to distort competition by favouring certain undertakings or the production of certain goods shall, in so far as it affects trade between Member States" as being in conflict with the treaty.[5]

215. The European Commission has provided guidance on how it will apply the State aid provisions in relation to direct business taxation.[6] According to this guidance an exception to a specific tax rule without any justification is considered State aid. However, the EU treaty provides EU Member States with options to introduce exceptions to the State aid provisions, for instance categories of State aid may be specified as being deemed compliant with the treaty.[7]

Notes

1. So far the Court of Justice of the European Union has not provided clarity on what significant influence means. In *Beker* (Case C-168/11) the Court highlighted that shareholding below 10% does not give a significant influence, and in *Itelcar* (Case C-282/12) and *Kronos* (Case C-47/12) the Court pointed out that shareholding above 10% does not necessarily imply that the holder exerts significant influence. In this respect, attention should also be given to other case law referred to in these decisions.
2. Council Directive 2003/123/EC of 22 December 2003 amending Directive 90/435/EEC on the common system of taxation applicable in the case of parent companies and subsidiaries of different Member States [2003] OJ L007/41.
3. Council Directive 2003/49/EC of 3 June 2003 on a common system of taxation applicable to interest and royalty payments made between associated companies of different Member States [2003] OJ L157/49.
4. *Scheuten Solar Technology* (Case C-397/09).
5. Article 107 of the Treaty on the Functioning of the European Union (TFEU).
6. Commission notice on the application of the State aid rules to measures relating to direct business taxation [1998] OJ C384/3.
7. Article 107(3)(e) TFEU.

Annex B

Data on companies affected by a benchmark fixed ratio at different levels

Table B.1 Tabulations for multinational and non-multinational companies, excluding companies with negative EBITDA, 2009-2013

Percentage of companies affected by interest deduction limitation

Percent of EBITDA limit on net interest deductibility	2009		2010		2011		2012		2013	
	Non-MNC	MNC	Non-MNC	MNC	Non-MNC	MNC	Non-MNC	MNC	Non-MNC	MNC
5%	59%	56%	57%	51%	57%	52%	57%	54%	56%	53%
10%	47%	41%	44%	35%	44%	37%	45%	39%	43%	38%
15%	37%	30%	34%	25%	35%	27%	36%	29%	34%	29%
20%	29%	23%	27%	19%	28%	20%	29%	23%	28%	23%
25%	24%	18%	22%	14%	23%	16%	25%	18%	22%	18%
30%	20%	14%	17%	11%	19%	13%	20%	15%	19%	14%
35%	16%	12%	14%	9%	16%	11%	17%	12%	16%	12%
40%	13%	9%	12%	7%	13%	9%	14%	11%	13%	10%
45%	11%	8%	9%	6%	11%	7%	12%	9%	11%	8%
50%	9%	7%	8%	5%	9%	6%	11%	8%	10%	7%
55%	8%	6%	7%	4%	8%	5%	9%	7%	9%	6%
60%	7%	5%	6%	4%	7%	4%	8%	6%	7%	6%
65%	6%	5%	5%	3%	6%	4%	7%	5%	7%	5%
70%	6%	4%	5%	3%	5%	4%	6%	5%	6%	5%
75%	5%	4%	4%	3%	5%	3%	5%	5%	6%	4%
80%	5%	3%	4%	2%	5%	3%	5%	4%	5%	4%
85%	4%	3%	4%	2%	4%	3%	5%	4%	5%	4%
90%	4%	3%	3%	2%	4%	3%	4%	3%	5%	3%
95%	4%	3%	3%	2%	3%	2%	4%	3%	4%	3%
100%	3%	3%	3%	2%	3%	2%	4%	3%	4%	3%
Observations	**6,472**	**10,911**	**6,675**	**11,372**	**6,631**	**11,165**	**6,547**	**11,015**	**6,523**	**10,908**

Source: PwC calculations based on consolidated financial statement information from Standard & Poor's GlobalVantage database.

Table B.2 Tabulations for multinational and non-multinational companies, excluding companies with negative EBITDA, average for 2009-2013

Percentage of companies affected by interest deduction limitation

Percent of EBITDA limit on net interest deductibility	Average 2009-2013	
	Non-MNC	MNC
5%	57%	53%
10%	45%	38%
15%	35%	28%
20%	28%	22%
25%	23%	17%
30%	19%	13%
35%	16%	11%
40%	13%	9%
45%	11%	8%
50%	9%	7%
55%	8%	6%
60%	7%	5%
65%	6%	4%
70%	6%	4%
75%	5%	4%
80%	5%	3%
85%	4%	3%
90%	4%	3%
95%	4%	3%
100%	3%	3%

Source: OECD Secretariat calculations based on data in Table B.1.

Table B.3 Tabulations for multinational and non-multinational companies, excluding companies with negative EBITDA, average for 2009-2013

Percentage of companies that would in principle be able to deduct an amount equivalent to their net third party interest expense

Percent of EBITDA limit on net interest deductibility	Average 2009-2013	
	Non-MNC	MNC
5%	43%	47%
10%	55%	62%
15%	65%	72%
20%	72%	78%
25%	77%	83%
30%	81%	87%
35%	84%	89%
40%	87%	91%
45%	89%	92%
50%	91%	93%
55%	92%	94%
60%	93%	95%
65%	94%	96%
70%	94%	96%
75%	95%	96%
80%	95%	97%
85%	96%	97%
90%	96%	97%
95%	96%	97%
100%	97%	97%

Source: OECD Secretariat calculations based on data in Table B.1.

Table B.2 includes the companies affected by a particular fixed ratio. Table B.3 includes the companies that in principle are not affected. Taken together, numbers from these tables for a particular ratio should add to 100%. Table B.3 assumes that net interest expense is spread around a group in accordance with EBITDA. In practice there may be barriers which prevent a group achieving this.

Table B.4 Tabulations for large cap and small cap multinational companies, excluding companies with negative EBITDA, 2009-2013

Percentage of multinational companies affected by interest deduction limitation

Percent of EBITDA limit on net interest deductibility	2009		2010		2011		2012		2013	
	Small Cap	Large Cap	Small Cap	Large Cap	Small Cap	Large Cap	Small Cap	Large Cap	Small Cap	Large Cap
5%	57%	56%	51%	51%	52%	48%	54%	53%	53%	54%
10%	42%	35%	36%	27%	37%	27%	40%	27%	39%	28%
15%	32%	20%	26%	15%	28%	15%	30%	16%	30%	17%
20%	24%	13%	20%	9%	21%	8%	24%	10%	24%	10%
25%	19%	8%	15%	5%	17%	5%	19%	6%	19%	7%
30%	15%	6%	12%	3%	14%	3%	16%	4%	15%	4%
35%	12%	4%	10%	2%	11%	2%	13%	2%	12%	3%
40%	10%	3%	8%	2%	9%	1%	11%	2%	10%	2%
45%	9%	3%	6%	1%	8%	1%	10%	1%	9%	1%
50%	7%	2%	5%	1%	7%	1%	8%	1%	8%	1%
55%	6%	2%	5%	0%	6%	0%	7%	1%	7%	1%
60%	6%	1%	4%	0%	5%	0%	6%	1%	6%	1%
65%	5%	1%	3%	0%	4%	0%	6%	1%	6%	1%
70%	4%	1%	3%	0%	4%	0%	5%	1%	5%	0%
75%	4%	1%	3%	0%	4%	0%	5%	0%	5%	0%
80%	4%	1%	3%	0%	3%	0%	4%	0%	4%	0%
85%	4%	0%	2%	0%	3%	0%	4%	0%	4%	0%
90%	3%	0%	2%	0%	3%	0%	4%	0%	4%	0%
95%	3%	0%	2%	0%	3%	0%	4%	0%	3%	0%
100%	3%	0%	2%	0%	3%	0%	3%	0%	3%	0%
Observations	**8,745**	**872**	**9,453**	**1,018**	**9,765**	**949**	**9,794**	**1,050**	**9,635**	**1,157**

Source: PwC calculations based on consolidated financial statement information from Standard & Poor's GlobalVantage database.

Annex C

The equity escape rule

216. The equity escape rule is currently applied by a number of countries, including Germany and Finland. The description below is based on the rule applied by Germany.

217. Under this approach, the fixed ratio rule does not apply to entities that are part of a group, if the entity can demonstrate that its equity/total assets ratio is equal to (within a tolerance of two percentage points) or higher than the equivalent group ratio. Where an entity's ratio is lower than that of the group, the entity remains subject to the fixed ratio rule. Under this approach, an entity which is leveraged more highly than its group cannot deduct interest expense up to its group's ratio.

218. For these purposes, a group exists if an entity may be consolidated with other entities under IFRS, or the financial or business decisions of the entity may be controlled together with those of other entities. A group also exists where entities are held or controlled by an individual or unincorporated entity.

219. The equity escape test should be based on audited consolidated financial statements of a group prepared in accordance with IFRS. However, audited financial statements drawn up in accordance with the commercial law of an EU Member State or US GAAP may be used if no IFRS financial statements are prepared. The requirement to prepare audited consolidated financial statements applies even where the group comprises entities under the control of an individual or unincorporated entity.

220. Entity financial statements should be prepared under the same accounting rules as the consolidated financial statements. Otherwise, a reconciliation must be prepared of the entity financial statements to the accounting standards used by the group, and this must be reviewed by an accountant. For purposes of determining the entity's equity ratio, all assets and liabilities must be valued using the same method as in the consolidated financial statements.

221. Therefore, an entity's equity figure must also be adjusted for the following items:

- to add goodwill included in the consolidated financial statements to the extent attributable to the business enterprise
- to adjust the valuation of assets and debts (valued at the amounts reported in the consolidated financial statements)
- to deduct equity not carrying voting rights (with the exception of preference shares)
- to deduct equity investments in other group entities.

222. An entity's total assets figure is adjusted for the following items:

- to add goodwill included in the consolidated financial statements to the extent attributable to the business enterprise
- to adjust the valuation of assets and debts (valued at the amounts reported in the consolidated financial statements)
- to deduct equity investments in other group entities
- to deduct financial claims which are not included in the consolidated financial statements but which are matched by liabilities of at least the same amount.

223. Anti-avoidance rules in Germany also require that, in applying the rule, an entity's equity and total assets figures are adjusted to deduct contributions made over the last six months prior to the relevant balance sheet date to the extent these are matched by withdrawals or distributions during the first six months after the relevant balance sheet date.

224. Even where the requirements of the equity escape rule are met, an entity which is part of a group remains subject to the fixed ratio rule unless the entity can demonstrate that interest payments on related-party loans from shareholders outside the group do not exceed 10% of the group's total net interest expense. A loan is a related party loan if it is from (i) a 25% shareholder (including direct and indirect shareholdings), (ii) an entity related to a shareholder, or (iii) any entity where there is recourse to a 25% shareholder.

Annex D

Examples

Example 1 – Thin capitalisation rule based on a fixed debt/equity ratio

225. A simple group structure includes two companies, Parent and Subsidiary. Subsidiary is resident in a country which applies a thin capitalisation rule based on a fixed debt/equity ratio of 1.5/1. In Year 1, Subsidiary has total debt from Parent of USD 750 million and total equity of USD 375 million.[1] On the intragroup debt, Subsidiary pays interest at a rate of 2%, or USD 15 million. As Subsidiary's debt/equity ratio of 2/1 exceeds the benchmark fixed ratio of 1.5/1, Subsidiary will incur an interest disallowance of USD 3.75 million. Subsidiary therefore has total interest deductions of USD 11.25 million.

226. To avoid this disallowance recurring, in Year 2 Subsidiary issues additional equity of USD 125 million to Parent. Subsidiary uses the funds received to make a loan to Parent of USD 125 million. The loan is on a short term basis at an interest rate of 1% and Subsidiary receives interest income of USD 1.25 million. Subsidiary's debt/equity ratio is now in line with the benchmark fixed ratio of 1.5/1 and so Subsidiary does not incur any interest disallowance. Subsidiary now has total net interest deductions of USD 13.75 million.

227. In Year 3, Subsidiary issues a further USD 100 million of equity and USD 150 million of debt to Parent. The new debt is on a medium term and bears interest at 2%. Subsidiary makes a new loan of USD 250 million to Parent on a short term basis at a rate of 1%. Subsidiary's debt/equity ratio is in line with the benchmark fixed ratio and Subsidiary incurs no interest disallowance. Subsidiary now has total net interest deductions of USD 14.25 million.

228. Finally, in Year 4, Subsidiary restructures USD 450 million of its existing debt into a long term subordinated loan with an arm's length interest rate of 5%. Subsidiary's debt/equity ratio is in line with the benchmark fixed ratio and Subsidiary incurs no interest disallowance. Subsidiary now has total net interest deductions of USD 27.75 million.

229. Between Year 1 and Year 4, Subsidiary's net interest deductions have increased from USD 11.25 million to USD 27.75 million, with no increase in underlying economic activity. Between Year 2 and Year 4, Subsidiary was fully compliant with the thin capitalisation rule based on a fixed debt/equity ratio.

230. However, this type of arrangement may contravene the general anti-avoidance rule of a country.

Example 2: Combining the best practice approach with other interest limitation rules

231. As set out in Chapter 1, a country may apply other interest limitation rules alongside those recommended in this report, either to tackle specific base erosion and profit shifting risks, or to achieve other tax policy goals. This is just one example of the way in which a country may apply the best practice approach alongside other rules but this is not the only approach available to countries.

232. In this example, Country X decides that a comprehensive approach to limiting an entity's interest deductions should comprise four parts. The first three of these are aimed at addressing base erosion and profit shifting involving interest. The fourth is included to achieve broader tax policy goals:

1. A fixed ratio rule which limits an entity's net interest deductions to 20% of EBITDA. This rule applies to all entities which are part of a multinational group or a domestic group. In this particular case, Country X does not apply the fixed ratio rule to standalone entities (although as stated in Chapter 3, a country may also choose to apply the fixed ratio rule to all entities, including standalone entities).
2. A group ratio rule, which allows an entity which is subject to the fixed ratio rule to deduct net interest expense up to the net third party interest/EBITDA ratio of its group, where this is higher than 20%.
3. Targeted rules to address specific base erosion and profit shifting risks involving interest. These rules are used to tackle base erosion and profit shifting risks involving interest posed by standalone entities. Some targeted rules are also used to prevent abuse of the general interest limitation rules by entities which are part of a multinational group or a domestic group.
4. An upper limit on the net interest expense of all entities (including all group entities and standalone entities) of 30% of EBITDA. This additional rule is not aimed at tackling base erosion and profit shifting involving interest but is used to reduce the existing tax bias in favour of debt funding over equity.

233. This approach is summarised in Table D.1 below.

Table D.1 How the best practice approach may be combined with other interest limitation rules

	Entities in multinational groups	Entities in domestic groups	Standalone entities
Fixed ratio rule (20% of EBITDA)	✓	✓	-
Group ratio rule	✓	✓	-
Targeted rules to address specific risks	✓	✓	✓
Upper limit on net interest deductions (30% of EBITDA)	✓	✓	✓

234. The application of these rules by Country X to five example companies is set out below.

Table D.2 Application of the best practice approach and other interest limitation rules

	A Co USD	B Co USD	C Co USD	D Co USD	E Co USD
EBITDA	100 million	100 million	100 million	100 million	100 million
Net interest expense	(15 million)	(28 million)	(33 million)	(30 million)	(35 million)
Group net third party interest/EBITDA ratio	10%	25%	35%	n/a	n/a

235. A Co is a company in a multinational group. A Co has net interest expense of USD 15 million and EBITDA of USD 100 million. Because A Co has a net interest/EBITDA ratio of below 20%, it is able to deduct all of its net interest expense. No targeted rules apply.

236. B Co is a company in a multinational group. B Co has net interest expense of USD 28 million and EBITDA of USD 100 million. Because B Co has a net interest/EBITDA ratio in excess of 20%, the fixed ratio rule would apply to restrict B Co's net interest deductions to USD 20 million. However, because B Co is part of a group which has a net third party interest/EBITDA ratio of 25%, B Co is able to apply the group ratio rule and deduct net interest expense of USD 25 million. USD 3 million of interest expense is disallowed. No targeted rules apply.

237. C Co is a company in a domestic group. C Co has net interest expense of USD 33 million and EBITDA of USD 100 million. Because C Co has a net interest/EBITDA ratio in excess of 20%, the fixed ratio rule would apply to restrict C Co's net interest deductions to USD 20 million. However, C Co is part of a group which has a net third party interest/EBITDA ratio of 35%, and so is able to apply the group ratio rule and deduct more net interest expense. Because the group ratio exceeds the upper limit on net interest deductions, C Co's net interest deductions are limited to 30% of EBITDA.

Therefore, C Co can deduct net interest expense of USD 30 million. USD 3 million of interest expense is disallowed. No targeted rules apply.

238. D Co is a standalone entity and is not part of any group. D Co is controlled by an individual who owns 100% of the ordinary shares in the company. D Co has net interest expense of USD 30 million and EBITDA of USD 100 million. This net interest expense includes USD 5 million paid on an arrangement giving rise to base erosion and profit shifting (such as an "artificial loan" where no new funding is raised by D Co). Because D Co is a standalone entity, it is not subject to the fixed ratio rule. Instead, D Co is subject to targeted rules which deal with the specific base erosion and profit shifting risks posed by standalone entities and to the upper limit on net interest deductions of 30% of EBITDA. Therefore, D Co is able to deduct USD 25 million of its net interest expense. USD 5 million is disallowed.

239. E Co is a standalone entity and is not part of any group. E Co has net third party interest expense of USD 35 million and EBITDA of USD 100 million. Because E Co is a standalone entity, it is not subject to the fixed ratio rule. However, it is subject to targeted rules to address specific base erosion and profit shifting risks (although none of those apply in this situation) and is also subject to the upper limit on net interest deductions of 30% of EBITDA. Therefore, E Co is able to deduct USD 30 million of its net interest expense. USD 5 million of interest expense is disallowed.

240. In introducing any interest limitation rules, or combination of rules, a country may need to take into account other legal or constitutional obligations. For example, countries which are EU Member States should consider the requirements of EU law.

Example 3: Interest and payments economically equivalent to interest

241. In 2015, A Co and its subsidiary B Co enter into the following arrangements:

1. A Co issues USD 50 million of bonds carrying a fixed interest rate of 5%.
2. A Co enters into an interest rate swap with a third party bank (Bank), under which A Co receives fixed rate payments and pays floating rate payments on a notional principal of USD 50 million.
3. B Co borrows USD 10 million from Bank at a floating interest rate.
4. B Co's borrowing from Bank is covered by a guarantee from A Co. In return, B Co pays a guarantee fee to A Co.
5. B Co also obtains a short term credit facility with Bank whereby it can borrow up to USD 500 000 for small periods at short notice. B Co pays an arrangement fee for this facility.
6. B Co enters into a finance lease for new plant and machinery for use in its business, payments under which include an interest element.
7. A Co enters into an operating lease for new office equipment.
8. B Co enters into a contract to provide 10 million widgets per year to Customer for the next three years. This contract is covered by a performance guarantee from A Co, in return for which B Co pays a guarantee fee to A Co.

9. B Co buys a series of aluminium futures contracts to protect itself against movements in the price of aluminium, a key ingredient in the manufacture of widgets.

10. A Co declares and pays a dividend of USD 1 million to holders of its ordinary shares.

242. The amounts payable by A Co and B Co under 1, 2, 3, 4, 5 and 6 are all interest on a debt, payments economically equivalent to interest, or expenses incurred in connection with the raising of finance. These payments are therefore subject to the fixed ratio rule and the group ratio rule. The amounts payable under 7, 8, 9 and 10 do not fall within these categories (based on this specific fact pattern) and are not subject to these rules.

Example 4: Fixed ratio rule (benchmark net interest/EBITDA ratio of 15%)

Table D.3 Operation of the fixed ratio rule

	Single entity taxation		Group taxation	
	A1 Co USD	A2 Co USD	Total USD	A1 Co + A2 Co USD
Taxable income/(losses) before applying the fixed ratio rule	70m	10m	80m	80m
+ net interest expense	+ 10m	+ 50m	+ 60m	+ 60m
+ depreciation and amortisation	+ 20m	+ 40m	+ 60m	+ 60m
= tax-EBITDA	= 100m	= 100m	= 200m	= 200m
x benchmark fixed ratio	x 15%	x 15%	-	x 15%
= maximum allowable deduction	= 15m	= 15m	-	= 30m
Disallowed interest expense	0	35m	35m	30m

243. In Table D.3, A1 Co and A2 Co incur a total disallowance of USD 30 million where the fixed ratio rule is applied at the level of the local group (e.g. under a group taxation regime). However, where they are taxed separately under a separate entity taxation regime, they incur a total disallowance of USD 35 million (which arises in A2 Co). This is because A1 Co is not fully utilising its capacity to absorb interest deductions and it is assumed that there are no rules in place to permit the surrender of interest capacity from A1Co to A2Co. The example illustrates the potential advantage of applying the rule at the level of the local group (although this may also be achieved if rules did allow the surrender of interest capacity within the group). However, depending on the individual situation of each group member the application of the rule at the group level may also be disadvantageous as shown in the example below.

Table D.4 Impact of losses on the operation of the fixed ratio rule

	Single entity taxation		Group taxation	
	A3 Co USD	A4 Co USD	Total USD	A3 Co + A4 Co USD
Taxable income/(losses) before applying the fixed ratio rule	100m	(150m)	(50m)	(50m)
+ net interest expense	+ 20m	+ 20m	+ 40m	+ 40m
+ depreciation and amortisation	+ 30m	+ 30m	+ 60m	+ 60m
= tax-EBITDA	= 150m	= (100m)	= 50m	= 50m
x benchmark fixed ratio	x 15%	x 15%	-	x 15%
= maximum allowable deduction	= 22.5m	= 0	-	= 7.5m
Disallowed interest expense	0	20m	20m	32.5m

244. Where one of the group entities is in a loss-making position and the fixed ratio rule is applied at the level of the local group, the total disallowance incurred is greater than if the rule would be applied at the level of each single entity. In Table D.4, A3 Co and A4 Co incur a total disallowance of USD 32.5 million where they are taxed under a group taxation regime. However, where they are taxed separately under a separate entity taxation regime, they incur a total disallowance of USD 20 million (which arises in A4 Co). This is because the loss in A4 Co partially reduces A3 Co's capacity to absorb interest deductions.

Example 5: Applying factors to set a benchmark fixed ratio within the corridor

245. As set out in Chapter 6, it is recommended that a country uses the factors in that chapter, along with other relevant factors, to set its benchmark fixed ratio within the recommended corridor of 10% to 30%. This example illustrates some possible ways in which this might be done, based on three countries which intend to introduce a fixed ratio rule: Country A, Country B and Country C. This is not meant to be an exhaustive list of possible approaches.

246. Country A considers each of the factors in Chapter 6:

1. It intends to introduce the fixed ratio rule alongside a group ratio rule.
2. It intends to allow entities to carry back disallowed interest expense for a period of three years.
3. It has no other tax rules which address the risks to be addressed by Action 4.
4. It does not have a high interest rate compared with other countries.
5. There is no legal or constitutional requirement for the same treatment to be applied to different types of entity.
6. It does not intend to apply different fixed ratios depending on the size of an entity's group.

247. In addition, Country A conducts its own analysis and concludes that groups operating in the country typically have low net third party interest/EBITDA ratios. Country A also wishes to apply a strict approach to tackle base erosion and profit shifting involving interest.

248. Country A determines that factors 1 to 5, as well as the additional factors, suggest a lower benchmark fixed ratio, while no factors suggest a higher ratio. Therefore, it concludes that it should set its benchmark fixed ratio towards the lower end of the corridor, within the illustrative range included in Figure D.1.

249. Country B considers each of the factors in Chapter 6:

1. It intends to introduce the fixed ratio alongside a group ratio rule.
2. It intends to allow entities to carry forward unused interest capacity without limitation.
3. It has other tax rules which specifically tackle a number of the risks to be addressed by Action 4 but not all of these risks.
4. It has a slightly high interest rate compared with other countries.
5. There is a legal requirement to apply the same fixed ratio to entities in multinational groups, entities in domestic groups and standalone entities.
6. It intends to apply one benchmark fixed ratio to entities in large groups, and a different benchmark fixed ratio to other entities.

250. Country B does not take into account any other factors in addition to the above.

251. Country B determines that two factors (1 and 2) suggest a lower benchmark fixed ratio, while three factors (3 to 5) suggest a higher benchmark fixed ratio. Country B also decides to apply a lower weighting to factors 3 and 4 because (i) although some of the base erosion and profit shifting risks to be addressed by Action 4 are dealt with by other tax rules, some of these risks remain, and (ii) although it has a slightly higher interest rate compared with other countries, this is not significantly higher.

252. Therefore, Country B concludes that it should not set its benchmark fixed ratio for most entities towards the top of the corridor, but rather within the illustrative range indicated in Figure D.1. In addition, recognising that large groups tend to have a lower net third party interest/EBITDA ratio than other groups, Country B decides to apply a lower ratio to entities in large groups.

253. Country C considers each of the factors in Chapter 6:

1. It intends to introduce the fixed ratio in isolation, without a group ratio rule.
2. It does not intend to allow entities to carry forward unused interest capacity or carry back disallowed interest expense.
3. It has other tax rules that tackle all of the issues to be addressed under Action 4.
4. It has a high interest rate compared with those of other countries.
5. There is a constitutional requirement to apply the same fixed ratio to entities in multinational groups, entities in domestic groups and standalone entities.
6. It does not intend to apply different fixed ratios depending on the size of an entity's group.

254. In addition, Country C applies a macro-economic policy to encourage third party lending not related to base erosion and profit shifting, to increase investment.

255. Country C determines that factors 1 to 5, as well as the additional factor, suggest a higher benchmark fixed ratio while no factors suggest a lower ratio. Therefore, it concludes that it may set its benchmark fixed ratio at any place in the corridor, from 10% to 30%.

Figure D.1 Applying factors to set a benchmark fixed ratio within the corridor

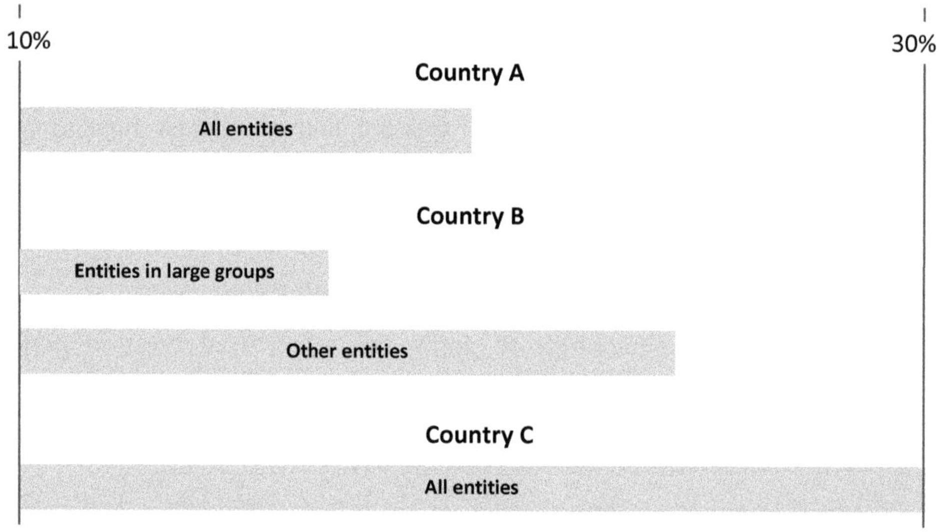

Example 6: Operation of a group ratio rule based on a net third party interest/EBITDA ratio

256. Examples 6a to 6c below illustrate how, in a simple case, a group ratio rule based on a net third party interest/EBITDA ratio could enable an entity which exceeds the benchmark fixed ratio to deduct more interest up to its group's net third party interest/EBITDA ratio.

257. In these examples, A Co is an entity resident in Country A. Country A applies a fixed ratio rule as described in Chapter 6, with a benchmark fixed ratio of 20%. A Co is part of a multinational group (Group). The net interest expense and EBITDA of A Co and Group are set out in the Table D.5.

Table D.5 Operation of a group ratio rule based on a net third party interest/EBITDA ratio

	Net interest expense USD	EBITDA USD
A Co	(10 million)	30 million
Group	(100 million)	400 million

Example 6a – Country A applies a fixed ratio rule in isolation

258. In this example, Country A applies a fixed ratio rule with a benchmark fixed ratio of 20%. Country A does not apply a group ratio rule.

259. A Co's interest capacity is calculated by applying the benchmark fixed ratio of 20% to its EBITDA of USD 30 million. A Co therefore has interest capacity of USD 6 million. Out of its total net interest expense of USD 10 million, USD 6 million may be deducted and USD 4 million is disallowed.

Example 6b – Country A applies a fixed ratio rule alongside a group ratio rule

260. In this example, Country A applies a fixed ratio rule with a benchmark ratio of 20%, and also a group ratio rule based on a net third party interest/EBITDA ratio. Under the group ratio rule, Country A does not apply any uplift to a group's net third party interest expense.

261. Under the fixed ratio rule, A Co's interest capacity is calculated by applying the benchmark fixed ratio of 20% to its EBITDA of USD 30 million. A Co therefore has interest capacity under the fixed ratio rule of USD 6 million.

262. Under the group ratio rule, A Co first calculates its group's net third party interest/EBITDA ratio, based on the group's net third party interest expense of USD 100 million and group EBITDA of USD 400 million. The group's ratio is therefore 25%. A Co applies the group ratio to its EBITDA of USD 30 million. A Co therefore has interest capacity under the fixed ratio rule of USD 7.5 million.

263. A Co's interest capacity is greater under the group ratio rule and so this rule applies. Out of A Co's total net interest expense of USD 10 million, USD 7.5 million may be deducted and USD 2.5 million is disallowed.

Example 6c – Country A applies a fixed ratio rule alongside a group ratio rule, with a 10% uplift to net third party interest expense

264. In this example, Country A applies a fixed ratio rule with a benchmark ratio of 20%, and also a group ratio rule based on a net third party interest/EBITDA ratio. Under the group ratio rule, Country A applies a 10% uplift to a group's net third party interest expense.

265. Under the fixed ratio rule, A Co's interest capacity is calculated by applying the benchmark fixed ratio of 20% to its EBITDA of USD 30 million. A Co therefore has interest capacity under the fixed ratio rule of USD 6 million.

266. Under the group ratio rule, A Co first calculates its group's net third party interest/EBITDA ratio. This is based on the group's adjusted net third party interest expense of USD 110 million (after applying an uplift of 10% to the group's actual net third party interest expense of USD 100 million) and group EBITDA of USD 400 million. The group's ratio is therefore 27.5%. A Co applies the group ratio to its EBITDA of USD 30 million. A Co therefore has interest capacity under the fixed ratio rule of USD 8.25 million.

267. A Co's interest capacity is greater under the group ratio rule and so this rule applies. Out of A Co's total net interest expense of USD 10 million, USD 8.25 million may be deducted and USD 1.75 million is disallowed.

Example 7: Definition of a group under a group ratio rule

268. The Examples 7a to 7e below show how a group is determined for the purposes of applying a group ratio rule, based on different fact patterns.

Example 7a – Companies held by an individual

Figure D.2 Companies held by an individual

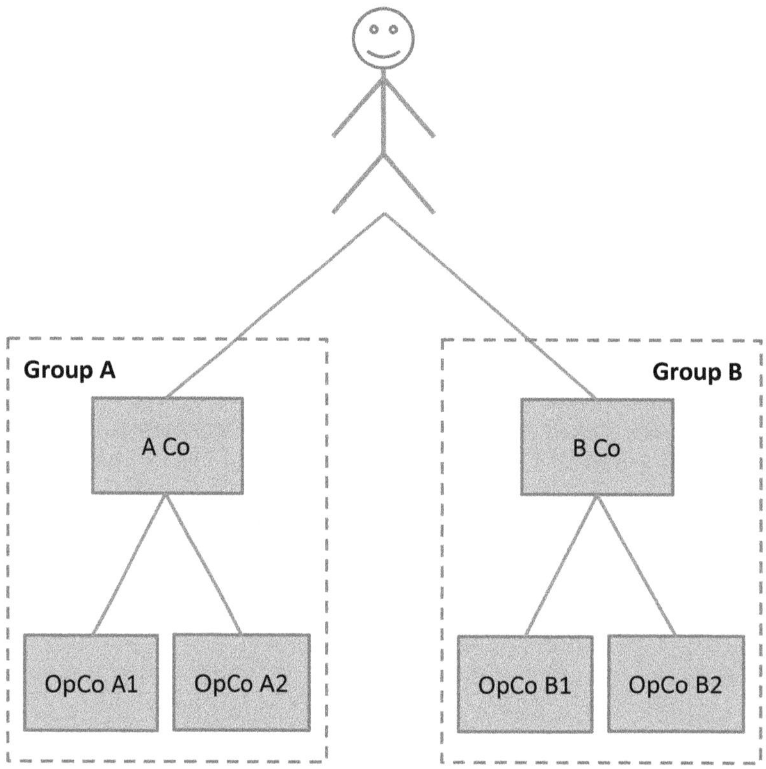

269. In Figure D.2, an individual owns the majority of the share capital in two companies, A Co and B Co, each of which has a number of subsidiaries. A Co and B Co are the top level company in their respective holding structures (i.e. no company exercises control over them). An individual cannot be the parent of a group. Therefore, for the purposes of applying the group ratio rule, two groups exist. Group A includes A Co and all entities included in A Co's consolidated financial statements, while Group B includes B Co and all entities included in B Co's consolidated financial statements.

270. In applying a group ratio rule, it is also necessary to identify which individuals and entities are related to a group, as this may be relevant in the calculation of the group's net third party interest expense. In this example, Group A is related to the individual, as well as to the entities in Group B. Similarly, Group B is related to the individual and to the entities in Group A.

Example 7b – Companies held by a limited partnership

271. Non-corporate vehicles such as limited partnerships cannot be the parent of a group for the purposes of a group ratio rule. A corporate group held under such a structure may be treated as a group, but this group will not include the limited partnership, any funds set up by the limited partnership to hold investments, or other corporate groups held under the structure. This is illustrated in Figure D.3, where Group A, Group B and Group C are treated as separate groups when applying a group ratio rule. However, the limited partnership, the sub-funds and Treasury Company would not form part of any group for these purposes.

Figure D.3 Companies held by a limited partnership

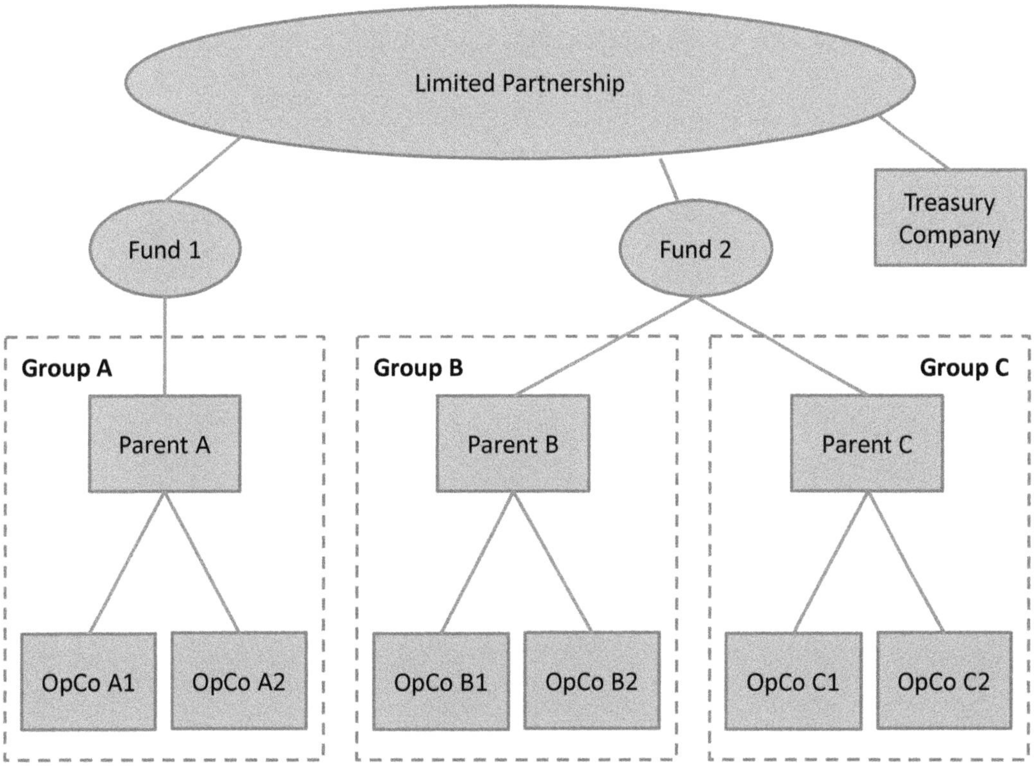

272. Although the limited partnership, the sub-funds and Treasury Company are not part of a group for group ratio rule purposes, they would be treated as related to each of Group A, Group B and Group C. Similarly, entities in each of the three groups would be treated as related to each other (so entities in Group A are related to entities in Group B and Group C, and so on).

Example 7c – Joint venture entity controlled by an investing group

Figure D.4 Joint venture entity controlled by an investing group

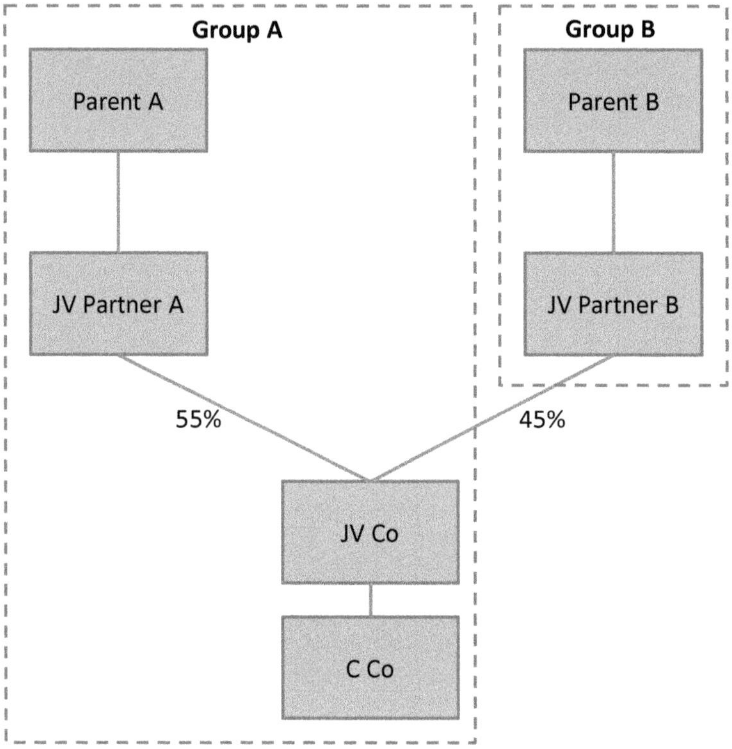

273. Where a joint venture entity is controlled by one of the joint venture partners, the joint venture entity will typically be included in the consolidated financial statements of the controlling group. It will therefore form part of this group for the purposes of applying a group ratio rule. This is shown in Figure D.4, where JV Partner A holds a 55% stake in JV Co. In this case, JV Co and its subsidiaries will be part of Group A for the purposes of applying a group ratio rule.

274. JV Partner B and JV Co are not part of the same group. However, JV Partner B holds an investment of greater than 25% in JV Co and so the two entities are related parties (as per the definition of related party in Chapter 9).

Example 7d - Joint venture entity which is not controlled by any investing group

Figure D.5 Joint venture entity which is not controlled by any investing group

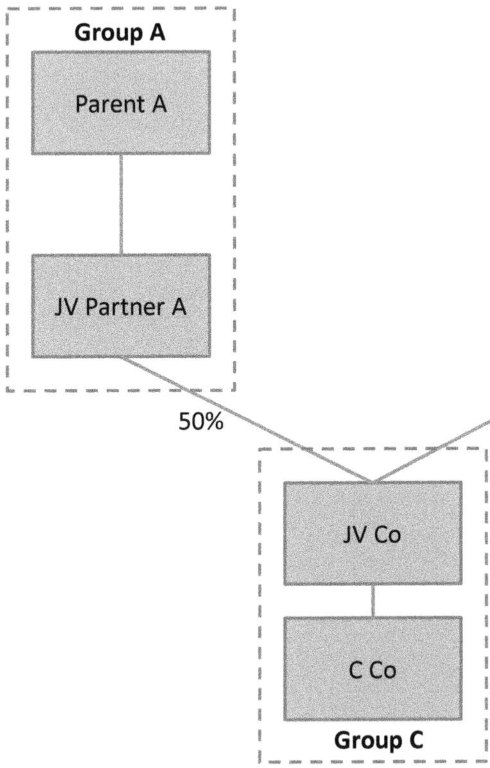

275. Where no investor has overall control of a joint venture entity, each investing group will generally include the joint venture in its consolidated financial statements using equity accounting. The joint venture entity is not consolidated into either investing group and will not form part of these groups for the purposes of a group ratio rule. This is shown in Figure D.5, where JV Partner A and JV Partner B each hold 50% stakes in JV Co, and no other arrangements exist which give control to one of the investors. JV Co and its subsidiary will not be part of either Group A or Group B. Instead, JV Co and its subsidiary will form a separate group (Group C). However, JV Co will be related to both JV Partner A and JV Partner B.

Example 7e – Holding structure headed by an investment entity

Figure D.6 Holding structure headed by an investment entity

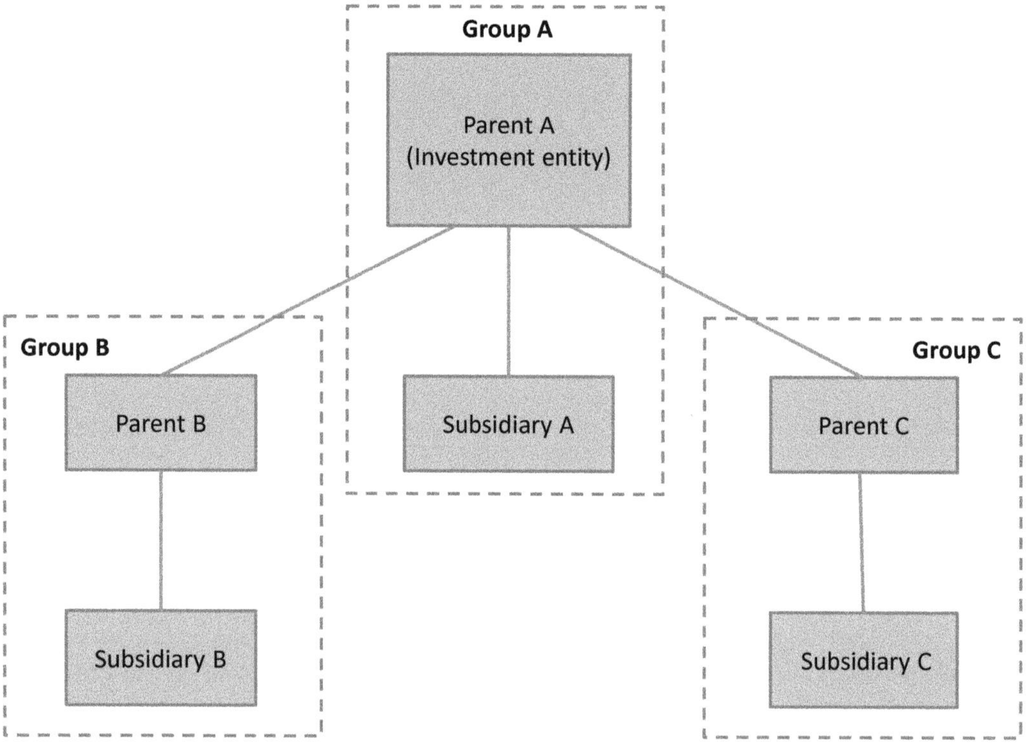

276. In Figure D.6, Parent A is a company which is an investment entity, and which directly controls three companies. Parent A is the top level company in the structure.

277. Subsidiary A provides services connected with Parent A's investment activities, and is consolidated into Parent A's consolidated financial statements.

278. Parent B and Parent C are held by Parent A for the purposes of capital appreciation and investment income. As such, they are recognised in Parent A's consolidated financial statements as investments and carried at fair value.

279. Parent A and Subsidiary A form a group (Group A) for the purposes of applying the group ratio rule. Parent B and Parent C are not members of Group A. Instead, each of these companies forms a separate group with their respective subsidiaries (Group B and Group C).

Example 8: Applying a group's ratio to an entity's tax-EBITDA or accounting-EBITDA

280. As set out in Chapter 7, when applying a group ratio rule an entity's EBITDA may be calculated using tax or accounting principles. Each of these approaches has advantages and disadvantages, which are considered in Examples 8a-8c below, based on the following scenario.

Table D.6 Applying a group's ratio to an entity's tax-EBITDA or accounting-EBITDA

	Financial reporting		Tax	
	Net interest expense USD	EBITDA USD	Net interest expense USD	EBITDA USD
Group	(100 million)	1 billion	n/a	n/a
A Co	(20 million)	100 million	(18 million)	80 million
Group net third party interest/EBITDA ratio = (USD 100 million / USD 1 billion) x 100 = 10%				

Example 8a - Determining EBITDA using tax principles

281. In this example, A Co's interest capacity is calculated by applying the group's net third party interest/EBITDA ratio of 10%, to A Co's tax-EBITDA of USD 80 million. This limit can be applied directly to A Co's net interest expense for tax purposes. Out of A Co's total net interest expense of USD 18 million, USD 8 million is tax deductible and USD 10 million is disallowed.

282. The calculation of EBITDA using tax principles is consistent with that recommended under the fixed ratio rule. It is also straightforward for groups to apply and tax authorities to audit, and as an approach to tackle base erosion and profit shifting it has the benefit that an entity's interest deductions are linked to its level of taxable income. This means that where an entity's taxable income is higher than its accounting income, its ability to deduct interest expense will be correspondingly greater. Similarly, if an entity undertakes planning to reduce its taxable income, it will be able to deduct less net interest expense.

Example 8b - Determining EBITDA using accounting principles

283. In this example, A Co's interest capacity is calculated by applying the group's net third party interest/EBITDA ratio of 10%, to A Co's accounting-EBITDA of USD 100 million. This limit can be applied directly to A Co's net interest expense for tax purposes. Out of A Co's total net interest expense of USD 18 million, USD 10 million is tax deductible and USD 8 million is disallowed.

284. Under this approach interest capacity is calculated using only accounting information. This is straightforward for groups to apply and tax authorities to audit. However, a possible concern remains if there is a significant difference between the calculation of net interest expense under tax and accounting rules. For example, an entity could incur a significant interest disallowance if the definition of interest it applies for tax purposes is wider than that for accounting purposes (because interest capacity has been calculated using the narrower accounting definition).

Example 8c – Adjusting an accounts-based limit on deductions for differences in tax and accounting definitions of interest

285. This example illustrates an approach to reduce the impact of differences between an entity's net interest expense for tax purposes and for accounting purposes. Under this

approach, the accounts-based limit on interest deductions calculated in Example 8b is compared with the entities net interest expense for accounting purposes, to determine what percentage falls within the limit. Where this figure is 100% (i.e. all of the entity's accounting net interest expense is within the limit), then all of the entity's net interest expense for tax purposes is deductible, with no disallowance. Where the percentage is less than 100%, the corresponding percentage of the entity's net interest expense for tax purposes is deductible, with the remainder disallowed (i.e. if 90% of the entity's accounting net interest expense falls within the limit, 90% of the entity's tax net interest expense would be deductible).

286. Applying this approach to A Co, the group's net third party interest/EBITDA ratio of 10% is applied to A Co's accounting-EBITDA of USD 100 million to produce an accounts-based limit on net interest expense of USD 10 million. This limit is compared with A Co's net interest expense for accounting purpose of USD 20 million, 50% of which falls within the limit. This percentage is then applied to A Co's net interest expense for tax purposes. Therefore, out of A Co's total net interest expense for tax purposes of USD 18 million, USD 9 million is deductible and USD 9 million is disallowed.

287. Compared with the accounts-based approach in Example 8b, this would mean, for example, where an entity's net interest expense for tax purposes exceeds that for accounting purposes, it would receive a correspondingly higher interest capacity. Alternatively, where an entity's net interest expense for tax purposes is lower than that for accounting purposes, its interest capacity would be reduced. In effect, the accounts-based limit on deductions is flexed to take into account differences between net interest expense for tax and accounting purposes.

Example 9: Dealing with loss-making entities within a group

Example 9a – The impact of losses on the operation of a group ratio rule

Table D.7 The impact of losses on the operation of a group ratio rule

	A Co USD	B Co USD	C Co USD	Group USD
EBITDA	100 million	10 million	(100 million)	10 million
Net interest	(20 million)	(2 million)	10 million	(12 million)
Group net third party interest/EBITDA ratio	-	-	-	120%
Interest capacity	120 million	12 million	0	-
Deductible interest expense	(20 million)	(2 million)	0	-
Disallowed interest expense	-	-	-	-
Unused interest capacity	100 million	10 million	-	-

288. In Table D.7, A Co has EBITDA of USD 100 million and net interest expense of USD 20 million. B Co has EBITDA of USD 10 million and net interest expense of USD 2 million. However, C Co has a negative EBITDA (i.e. losses) of USD 100 million and receives net interest income of USD 10 million. Therefore, looking at the group as a whole, the group has total EBITDA of USD 10 million and a net interest expense of USD 12 million. The group's net third party interest/EBITDA ratio is 120%.

289. This very high group ratio causes two problems. Firstly, in the current year A Co receives interest capacity of USD 120 million, which is higher than the group's actual net third party interest expense. This means that in principle the company could deduct more net interest than the total net third party interest expense of the group. Secondly, even after deducting their current year net interest expense, A Co and B Co still have a high level of unused interest capacity. If a rule allows the carry forward of unused interest capacity, this could be carried into future periods and used to shelter further interest deductions.

290. In a sense, this issue arises because C Co (which has a negative EBITDA of USD 100 million) is not required to recognise negative interest capacity of USD 120 million. If this was the case, then the interest capacity of the group as a whole would equal the group's net third party interest expense of USD 12 million. However, the recognition of negative interest capacity in loss-making entities is not recommended as part of the best practice approach.

Example 9b – Applying an upper limit on interest capacity

Table D.8 Applying an upper limit on interest capacity

	A Co USD	B Co USD	C Co USD	Group USD
EBITDA	100 million	10 million	(100 million)	10 million
Net interest	(20 million)	(2 million)	10 million	(12 million)
Group net third party interest/EBITDA ratio	-	-	-	120%
Interest capacity	12 million	12 million	0	-
Deductible interest expense	(12 million)	(2 million)	0	-
Disallowed interest expense	(8 million)	-	-	-
Unused interest capacity	-	10 million	-	-

291. In Table D.8, the group is in the same position as in Example 9a. However, the interest capacity of A Co is now subject to limitation equal to the group's actual net third party interest expense. Therefore, A Co's interest capacity is limited to USD 12 million (i.e. the group's total net third party interest expense). A Co is able to deduct net interest expense of USD 12 million, and may carry forward disallowed interest expense of USD 8 million into future periods, if this is permitted under a rule.

292. As before, B Co receives interest capacity of USD 12 million and is able to deduct its full net interest expense of USD 2 million. It is also able to carry forward unused interest capacity of USD 10 million, if this is permitted by a country's rule. As discussed in in Chapter 7, it is suggested that countries consider limiting the scope of any carry forward, and in particular those of unused interest capacity, by time and/or value.

293. Note that if the group's EBITDA had not been reduced by losses in C Co, the group's net third party interest/EBITDA ratio would have been approximately 10.9% (i.e. USD 12 million/USD 110 million). In this case, A Co would have been able to deduct approximately USD 10.9 million of net interest expense. Therefore, the upper limit on interest capacity has not restricted net interest deductions in A Co to below the level that would have been permitted had the losses in C Co not arisen.

Example 9c – Groups with negative consolidated EBITDA

Table D.9 Groups with negative consolidated EBITDA

	A Co USD	B Co USD	C Co USD	Group USD
EBITDA	100 million	10 million	(120 million)	(10 million)
Net interest	(20 million)	(2 million)	10 million	(12 million)
Group net third party interest/EBITDA ratio	-	-	-	n/a
Interest capacity	12 million	2 million	0	-
Deductible interest expense	(12 million)	(2 million)	0	-
Disallowed interest expense	(8 million)	-	-	-
Unused interest capacity	-	-	-	-

294. In Table D.9, Co has losses of USD 120 million. The group has an overall loss (negative consolidated EBITDA) of USD 10 million, which means it is not possible to calculate a meaningful group ratio. A Co and B Co therefore receive interest capacity equal to the lower of their net interest expense and the group's net third party interest expense.

295. A Co has net interest expense of USD 20 million, which exceeds the group's net third party interest expense of USD 12 million. A Co's interest capacity is therefore USD 12 million. A Co is able to deduct net interest expense of USD 12 million, and may carry forward disallowed interest expense of USD 8 million into future periods, if this is permitted.

296. B Co has net interest expense of USD 2 million, which is lower than the group's net third party interest expense of USD 12 million. B Co's interest capacity is therefore USD 2 million. B Co may deduct its entire interest expense of USD 2 million. There is no unused interest capacity.

Example 9d – Excluding loss-making entities from the calculation of group EBITDA for a profitable group

Table D.10 Excluding loss-making entities from the calculation of group EBITDA for a profitable group

	A Co USD	B Co USD	C Co USD	Group USD
EBITDA	100 million	10 million	(100 million)	110 million
Net interest	(20 million)	(2 million)	10 million	(12 million)
Group net third party interest/EBITDA ratio	-	-	-	10.9%
Interest capacity	10.9 million	1.1 million	0	-
Deductible interest expense	(10.9 million)	(1.1 million)	0	-
Disallowed interest expense	(9.1 million)	(0.9 million)	-	-
Unused interest capacity	-	-	-	-

297. This example is based on the same fact pattern as Example 9a. In this case, the negative EBITDA in C Co has been disregarded in calculating the group's EBITDA. Therefore, the group now has EBITDA of USD 110 million, rather than USD 10 million. This means that the group's interest/EBITDA ratio is now reduced to 10.9%.

298. The effect of this is that A Co has interest capacity of USD 10.9 million and B Co has interest capacity of USD 1.1 million. These total USD 12 million, which is equal to the group's net third party interest expense. By disregarding C Co's losses, the group ratio rule now operates to ensure that the group is able to deduct an amount equal to its actual net third party interest expense. However, it may be very difficult for the tax authorities in the countries of A Co and B Co to accurately establish the existence and value of the negative EBITDA in C Co. Therefore, it may not be feasible for a country to apply this approach in practice.

Example 9e – Excluding loss-making entities from the calculation of group EBITDA for a loss-making group

Table D.11 Excluding loss-making entities from the calculation of group EBITDA for a loss-making group

	A Co USD	B Co USD	C Co USD	Group USD
EBITDA	100 million	10 million	(120 million)	110 million
Net interest	(20 million)	(2 million)	10 million	(12 million)
Group net third party interest/EBITDA ratio	-	-	-	10.9%
Interest capacity	10.9 million	1.1 million	0	-
Deductible interest expense	(10.9 million)	(1.1 million)	0	-
Disallowed interest expense	(9.1 million)	(0.9 million)	-	-
Unused interest capacity	-	-	-	-

299. This example is based on the same fact pattern as in Example 9c. However, in this case the negative EBITDA in C Co is disregarded in calculating the group's EBITDA. Therefore, rather than being unable to calculate a meaningful group net third party interest/EBITDA ratio, the group now has a net third party interest/EBITDA ratio of 10.9%.

300. A Co now has interest capacity of USD 10.9 million and B Co has interest capacity of USD 1.1 million. In total, these come to USD 12 million, which is equal to the group's net third party interest expense. By disregarding C Co's losses, the group is able to deduct an amount equal to its actual net third party interest expense. However, in practice it may be very difficult for the tax authorities in the countries of A Co and B Co to accurately establish the existence and value of the negative EBITDA in C Co.

Example 10: Fixed ratio rule using EBITDA based on a three year average

301. Table D.12 illustrates how the negative impact of a temporary fall in profits under a fixed ratio rule may be mitigated through the use of a three year moving average of the EBITDA of an entity.

Table D.12 Fixed ratio rule using EBITDA based on a three year average

	Year (current tax year = t)					
	t-2 USD	t-1 USD	t USD	t+1 USD	t+2 USD	t+3 USD
Using current year tax-EBITDA						
Taxable income before applying the fixed ratio rule	380m	350m	100m	300m	320m	300m
+ net interest expense	+ 100m	+ 100m	+ 100m	+ 100m	+ 100m	+ 100m
+ depreciation and amortisation	+ 50m	+ 50m	+ 50m	+ 50m	+ 50m	+ 50m
= tax-EBITDA	= 530m	= 500m	= 250m	= 450m	= 470m	= 450m
x benchmark fixed ratio	x 30%	x 30%	x 30%	x 30%	x 30%	x 30%
= maximum allowable deduction	= 159m	= 150m	= 75m	= 135m	= 141m	= 135m
Disallowed interest expense	0	0	25m	0	0	0
Using three year average tax-EBITDA						
Average tax-EBITDA of current year + 2 previous years			427m	400m	390m	457m
x benchmark fixed ratio			x 30%	x 30%	x 30%	x 30%
= maximum allowable deduction			= 128m	= 120m	= 117m	= 137m
Disallowed interest expense	0	0	0	0	0	0

302. In the upper part of the table the excessive interest is calculated by using the current year tax-EBITDA. In year t the entity suffers a temporary fall in profits and as a result USD 25 million of interest expense is non-deductible. The entity may be able to carry forward this disallowed interest expense for use in future periods, if this is permitted. The lower part of the table illustrates the effect of using the moving average

tax-EBITDA of the last three years to calculate the maximum allowable interest deduction. As a result of using the three year average the temporary fall in profits is spread over a three year period. The impact of this is that the entity is able to deduct all of its interest expense in year t, and has a lower maximum allowable deduction in years t+1 and t+2 compared to the base case.

Notes

1. All monetary amounts in this annex are denominated in United States dollars (USD). These are illustrative examples only, and are not intended to reflect real cases or the position in a particular country.

ORGANISATION FOR ECONOMIC CO-OPERATION AND DEVELOPMENT

The OECD is a unique forum where governments work together to address the economic, social and environmental challenges of globalisation. The OECD is also at the forefront of efforts to understand and to help governments respond to new developments and concerns, such as corporate governance, the information economy and the challenges of an ageing population. The Organisation provides a setting where governments can compare policy experiences, seek answers to common problems, identify good practice and work to co-ordinate domestic and international policies.

The OECD member countries are: Australia, Austria, Belgium, Canada, Chile, the Czech Republic, Denmark, Estonia, Finland, France, Germany, Greece, Hungary, Iceland, Ireland, Israel, Italy, Japan, Korea, Luxembourg, Mexico, the Netherlands, New Zealand, Norway, Poland, Portugal, the Slovak Republic, Slovenia, Spain, Sweden, Switzerland, Turkey, the United Kingdom and the United States. The European Union takes part in the work of the OECD.

OECD Publishing disseminates widely the results of the Organisation's statistics gathering and research on economic, social and environmental issues, as well as the conventions, guidelines and standards agreed by its members.

OECD PUBLISHING, 2, rue André-Pascal, 75775 PARIS CEDEX 16
(23 2015 31 1 P) ISBN 978-92-64-24116-9 – 2015

www.ingramcontent.com/pod-product-compliance
Ingram Content Group UK Ltd.
Pitfield, Milton Keynes, MK11 3LW, UK
UKHW051507290926
15471UKWH00008B/1464

9 789264 241169